Why Do Bad Things Happen to Good People?

Why Do Bad Things Happen to Good People?

A Biblical look at
the problem of suffering

MELVIN TINKER

CHRISTIAN
FOCUS

Melvin Tinker is Vicar of St John's Newland in Hull. He read theology at Oxford and trained for ordination at Wycliffe Hall, before becoming a curate at Wetherby Parish Church in Yorkshire. Prior to his current position he was Anglican Chaplain to the University of Keele in Staffordshire. He has written on a wide variety of subjects relating to doctrine and ethics. He has written *Close Encounters* (ISBN 978-1-85792-123-8), *Alien Nation* (ISBN 978-1-85792-677-4) and *Road to Reality - finding meaning in a meaningless world* (ISBN 978-1-85792-958-4) and *Tales of the Unexpected - The Subversive stories of Jesus* (ISBN 978-1-84550-116-7). Melvin is married to Heather and they have three boys.

© Melvin Tinker
ISBN 978-1-85792-322-3

10 9 8 7 6 5 4 3 2 1

First published in 1997,
reprinted in 2000, 2004, 2005, 2006 and 2009
by
Christian Focus Publications Ltd.,
Geanies House, Fearn,
Ross-shire, IV20 1TW, Great Britain

www.christianfocus.com

Cover Design by Moose77.com

Printed and Bound by
Norhaven A/S, Denmark

Contents

Foreword 7

Preface 9

1. The Big Picture 13

2. What's Happening? (Job 1–3) 39

3. With Friends Like These ... (Job 4–31) 55

4. God Has Spoken (Job 32–41) 71

5. All's Well that Ends Well (Job 42) 85

6. A Very Peculiar Form of Suffering (Psalm 42).... 97

7. It's Not Fair (Psalm 73) 111

8. What Does Jesus Say? (Luke 13:1-5). 123

9. Saintly Suffering (1 Peter 4:12-19).............. 135

10. The Big Picture Revisited (Revelation 5)...... 147

*This book is dedicated with gratitude
to my parents.*

FOREWORD

Throughout my own attempts to share the Christian Faith with others the one question that comes up more than any other is the title of this book, 'Why do bad things happen to good people?' or as it's sometimes put: 'How in a world of suffering can you believe in a God of Love? Why do people suffer?' These are timeless and universal questions to which there are no simple answers. However, the Christian faith stands out from all the other religions in the world, and sheds unique light on this question and enables us to explore it with new perspectives.

Melvin Tinker in this lucid and relevant book leads us in the exploration. He is widely read and shows how the Bible offers us insights that are both authoritative and contemporary. Melvin is also a pastor and comes to the question with all the sensitivity of one who has come alongside those who suffer and has heard their cries and their questionings.

Throughout these pages he never loses sight of the two sides of the coin – God is Love and God is omnipotent. As with a coin it is difficult to see both sides at once; so when we suffer it can be hard to believe both truths about God – that he is both all loving and all powerful. The dominant theme of this book is the sovereignty of God which the author offers as the key doctrine to coming to terms both theoretically and pastorally with the reality of suffering.

Melvin writes in a style that draws the reader into the argument always anticipating the question of the reader. Although these chapters are easy to read (Melvin is a gifted teacher both in the pulpit and on the written page) the reader will find the arguments strong meat, not least chapter eight. I encourage you to approach this subject prayerfully. Theology without prayer is but an academic exercise; with prayer it becomes the means of knowing God and his will for our lives.

More than ever in our recent history the church needs to equip the followers of Jesus to face the questions that seekers after truth and faith are asking. This book is a valuable tool for all Christians wanting to think through their faith for themselves and for the sake of others.

The Right Reverend James Jones,
Bishop of Liverpool

Preface

Switch on the TV, pick up a newspaper, listen to the radio, and there will be at least one item dealing with tragedy – a murder, a train crash, a well-known celebrity struck down in her prime with cancer. It is a sad, sick world causing many to ask the questions: 'Why? If there is a good God, why does he permit such things to happen? Can't he *do something? Doesn't he care?*'

Of course, from one point of view there can never be a full explanation in answer to the question 'Why?' The nature of evil is such that it inhabits that sphere of our existence which is dark and impenetrable to reason. Pastorally, the call is often simply to 'weep with those who weep' and to offer practical, loving support, including our prayers. Also we need to foster, as much as is humanly possible, the conditions which minimise the occurrence of such horrors. Nevertheless, while a total explanation of these and similar events (including more 'natural tragedies') may not be possible, the Christian believes that God has spoken and acted in such a way that some understanding, however tentative, lies within our grasp.

The Bible is a realistic book, dealing with the way things are and not merely as we would like them to be. What is more, the Bible makes the amazing claim that the One who created this world entered into it as a baby in Bethlehem and died as a young man on a cross in Golgotha. The Nazarene, Jesus, was 'Emmanuel', meaning 'God with us'. In other words, God knows from the 'inside' what suffering is. Therefore, it would be very surprising indeed if the Bible were found to be silent on this matter of the 'problem of pain'. As we shall see, the Bible is far from silent; it provides penetrating insight into the whole question of evil and suffering which is without parallel. While what is given may not be exhaustive, the Christian believes it is sufficient (2 Tim. 3:16f.).

The purpose of this book is not to give the answer to the problem of evil in general or suffering in particular, but, rather by a combination of a biblical overview and Bible exposition, to indicate practical ways by which we may come to terms with living in a broken, suffering world against the backdrop of God's greater sovereign purposes.

The first chapter attempts to provide the overview, indicating one way of perceiving the question of suffering which I believe is true to the Bible's main emphasis. This chapter is doctrinal in nature and touches on some philosophical questions. While the following chapters can be read independently of the opening section, it is worth wrestling with it in order to have a wider framework within which one can place the rest.

There then follows a series of expositions designed to uncover the meaning of certain biblical texts as well as to drive home their application for us today. Not surprisingly, the book of Job receives extensive treatment, it being the most well-known story from the Scriptures which specifically addresses the problem of innocent suffering 'head on', albeit in poetic form. Then, having considered one special form of suffering (spiritual depression), we turn to some key New Testament passages which highlight the dominant themes of the whole Bible on the question of suffering. Vitally important in this regard is Jesus' teaching in Luke 13 which tends to be largely neglected.

This book tries to tread the difficult path of affirming with Scripture the sovereignty of God without, at the same time, trivialising the suffering of man. It is firmly believed that this God who is sovereign over all (including our 'losses and crosses' as the Puritans would say) is our ultimate source of comfort and, therefore, hope. One early Christian writer, offering wisdom and comfort to his congregations undergoing tremendous suffering for their faith, summarises this position well when he wrote: 'For we do not have a high priest who is unable to sympathise (literally, 'suffer

11

with') our weaknesses, but we have one who has been tempted in every way, just as we are – yet was without sin. Let us then approach the throne of grace with confidence, so that we may receive mercy and find grace to help us in our time of need' (Heb. 4:15, 16).

Melvin Tinker,
St John's Newland, Hull.
Soli Deo Gloria.

Chapter 1

THE BIG PICTURE

On the 1st of November, 1755, Lisbon was devastated by an earthquake. Being All Saints Day, the churches were packed to capacity and thirty of them were destroyed. Within six minutes 15,000 people had died and another 15,000 lay dying. This was the eighteenth century equivalent to a nuclear holocaust, but one not caused by the perversity of man.

One of the many thinkers horrified by this event was the French philosopher Voltaire. His cry was quite simply: how could anyone believe in a benevolent and omnipotent God after this? What else could he do but treat with scorn Alexander Pope's lines in his *Essay on Man*, written from a comfortable villa in Twickenham:

> And, spite of pride, in erring reason's spite,
> One truth is clear, Whatever is, is right.

This, for Voltaire, was the crass poetic expression of the philosophy of Optimism – a philosophy which just over 150 years later, in a different guise, was itself to be cut to ribbons in the form of the bodies of those young men who died on the battlefields of the Somme and Paschendale. In protest Voltaire railed against such optimism in his *Poem on the Disaster of Lisbon*, which asked: if God is free, just and benevolent, why do we suffer under his rule? Later, similar thoughts were to find expression in the satirical novel *Candide,* whose teacher Dr Pangloss, a Professor of Optimism, blandly assures him that 'all is for the best in the best of all possible worlds'. Later, after many more disasters, not least the hanging of Dr Pangloss by the Inquisition, Voltaire writes: 'Candide, terrified speechless, bleeding, palpitating said to himself :"If this is the best of all possible worlds, what can the rest be?" '

While neither the Bible, nor any Christian theology founded upon the Bible, ever claims that this is the best of all possible worlds, one must at least sympathise with the sentiments that Voltaire is giving voice to, namely, that at the very least there is an apparent contradiction between belief in an all-powerful, loving God and the fact of suffering which is deemed evil. Therefore, it is common to speak of the 'problem' of evil or the 'problem' of suffering.

However, it ought to be made clear at the outset that for the atheist or the thorough-going materialist, there isn't a problem of evil in that evil and suffering do not count against his beliefs. For the atheist/materialist suffering is a mere fact of existence, a datum of experience like the redness of red or the wetness of water. It may be a problem for the atheist in that he, like the rest of us, has to cope with the unpleasantness of suffering or struggle against the threat of annihilation which would render all his efforts ultimately meaningless, but as far as his belief system goes it is not significantly brought into question by suffering *per se*.

THE DILEMMA FORMULATED

For the Christian, however, suffering and evil do pose a problem because of what he or she believes. So McClosky writes:

> Evil is a problem for the theist in that a contradiction is involved in the fact of evil, on the one hand, and the belief in the omnipotence of God on the other.[1]

Or the problem may be put in the form of a dilemma as formulated by John Hick:

> If God is perfectly loving and good he must wish to abolish evil; if God is all powerful he must be able to abolish evil. But evil exists, therefore God cannot be both perfectly good and almighty.[2]

Even if some of the terms Hick uses here were to be qualified so that 'good' is to be distinguished from sentimental indulgence and were to incorporate, as

---

1. N. Pike, ed. *God and Evil* (Prentice Hall, 1964).
2. John Hick, 'An Irenean Theodicy', *Encountering Evil*, S. T. Davies, ed. (T&T Clark, 1981).

the Bible insists must be the case, God's righteous anger towards wrong; and omnipotence were to be defined in a way that did not involve the ability to do that which was self-contradictory – as distinct from antinomies (for example, the old chestnut, can God make a boulder so large that he cannot move it?) – we have to admit honestly that *prima facie* there is a dilemma which needs to be addressed.

Let us focus, therefore, on this particular formulation of the dilemma: if God is good he must wish to abolish evil; if he is omnipotent he must be able to abolish evil; but evil exists and so he cannot be both all powerful and good.

A moment's reflection upon this conundrum soon reveals two things which this dilemma presupposes for it to be effective. The first presupposition is that if God is good and all powerful he must wish to abolish evil now, or at least it raises the questions why he didn't remove it earlier or why he allowed it to come into being in the first place. The second presupposition is that he must do it in an immediate and total way, presumably by divine fiat. In other words, there is both a temporal and a means condition built in to the formulation.

But what if it could be demonstrated, however tentatively, that God will not only deal with evil at some point in the *future,* but that he will in some measure 'redeem' its consequences by a means we would not think of and in a way that will transfigure it in to that which is good? What is more, what if it could be demonstrated that God has *already* done something to deal with evil? Then some, but by no means all, of the force is taken out of the dilemma. The tension would be relieved but not entirely resolved.

SIMPLE SOLUTIONS

There are, of course, some simple solutions to the dilemma which essentially involve the removal of one or more of the elements of belief so it ceases to be a dilemma at all.

One could deny the existence of evil or suffering, viewing them as 'illusory' – Theravada Buddhism or Christian Science might qualify as examples here. Alternatively, one could deny that God is all-powerful, as does the Process theologian David Griffin who states quite unashamedly that his solution is found by 'denying the doctrine of omnipotence fundamental to it.'[3] Or thirdly, one could deny the goodness of God, a view well captured by Archibald MacLeish in his play *JB*, an updated presentation of the story of Job in which one finds the haunting refrain: 'If he is God he is not good, if he is good he is not God.'

The traditional Christian claim, however, is that God is good and almighty, and that evil and suffering are realities to be reckoned with. The 'problem' therefore turns on how to relate these two articles

---

3. David Griffin, 'Creation out of Chaos and the Problem of Evil', *Encountering Evil*, S. T. Davies, ed. (T&T Clark, 1981).

of faith (the goodness and omnipotence of God) to the fact of suffering, without compromising either of these tenets of belief or trivialising human pain.

THE MORAL STATUS OF PAIN

In turning to consider the question: 'What makes suffering morally unacceptable?', a prior question needs to be addressed: 'Is all suffering evil or is it evil only within certain contexts?' While psychologically most pain might be considered to be objectionable, it is not necessarily the case that it is morally so, especially if the pain endured is part of the means to a recognised good end. For example, biologically, pain serves as part of the body's defence mechanism preventing further injury by means of, say, a reflex action. Certainly it could be objected that this simply pushes the 'problem' one stage back, for one could ask, 'Why the more serious injury?' Even so, the point still remains that pain in itself is not necessarily evil. In some contexts it is morally neutral, like the 'healthy' pain after long exercise, or morally good, as in the case of corrective punishment.

Surely, what makes suffering so morally objectionable is when it is encountered in a form which is wholly negative, apparently devoid of any significance. It is this which lies at the root of so many tormented human cries – 'Why should my ten-day-old baby die?' 'Why should such a gifted man be reduced to a mere shell through Alzheimers?' It is this seeming lack of purpose, what is often referred to as dysteleological suffering, that provides the twist which calls for such pain to be viewed as evil. And so we might put the matter like this: that suffering 'becomes' morally unacceptable when, within our own limited temporal context, it exhibits those features commonly recognised as standing in direct opposition to that which is good – for example, disintegration and meaninglessness.

This particular perspective on the nature of evil has been pursued to great effect by Karl Barth.[4] Following through Augustine's contention of evil as *privatio boni* (the deprivation of the good which has no independent existence, so evil takes on the character of a parasite, for example, gluttony is an abuse of the 'good' of eating), Barth conceives of evil as 'das Nichtige' – 'nothingness, an impossible possibility', that which God saw fit to pass over. Such categories of description are used to convey the essential negative nature of evil. This immediately introduces us to the inevitable paradox and limitations in the use of language in describing that which is the metaphysical equivalent to 'anti-matter', without at the same time giving the false impression that evil is somehow an illusion. In spite of claims to the contrary, this analysis of Barth maintains that evil is a reality, a negative reality, the 'surd' which has no creative purpose. As such it acquires 'anti-qualities' and so is deemed evil.

---

4.   Karl Barth, *Church Dogmatics* III, pp. 289-363, (T&T Clark).

THE WHY OF SUFFERING

When one asks the question 'Why is there suffering?' one could be straining towards one of two things. First, one could be looking for a cause: 'What is the cause of suffering?'; both in terms of an ultimate cause: 'Where did it come from in the first place?', or, in the more immediate sense, a proximal cause: 'What is the cause of this particular suffering?'

This general line of approach to the question of evil has many distinguished writers to commend it – Augustine, C. S. Lewis, Alvin Plantinga, to name but three. Here explanations are sought in terms of free will defence, the Fall, the activity of fallen angels and so on. Each of these has some part to play in moving towards an overall Christian understanding of suffering and evil in the world.

It is the teaching about the Fall which is particularly significant and foundational.[5] The basic outline of the biblical plot is that the sovereign and totally good God created a good universe. We human beings rebelled and that rebellion is now such a part of our make-up that we are enmeshed in it. All the suffering we now face turns on this fact, and in some way is related to 'sin' (but not all suffering is related to sin in the same way). The Bible centres on how God takes action to reverse these terrible effects and their root cause which is sin itself. Furthermore, the

---

5. See D. A. Carson, *How Long O Lord?* (IVP, 1990) for an excellent development of the biblical picture.

believer sees on the broader canvas the future dimension of a new heaven and earth where neither sin nor sorrow will ever be experienced again.

This means that there is a fundamental recognition by the Christian that the world in which we live is thrown out of joint at every level – it is not the best of all possible worlds, far from it. The price of sin is great, and suffering in this life is in some measure a consequence of sin. Indeed, this is a world well-suited to sinners, the discomfort reminding us that all is not well in our relations with our Maker. Whereas the cry of our post-Enlightenment generation, echoing the cry of a man like Voltaire, is 'How can God be so cruel?', the cry of earlier generations was one with a man like Martin Luther asking, 'How can God be so merciful?' The reason why we find it so difficult to utter the latter (but not hard to pronounce the former) is because we fail to appreciate the seriousness of sin and the pure character of a God who stands in opposition to sin.

Nevertheless, this is not to say that every item of suffering is the *immediate* cause of sin. As we shall see, Jesus clearly corrects that idea, for it is patently obvious that many 'good people' do suffer. What is more, Christians of all people should certainly not expect a trouble-free life; they have their 'losses and crosses' as the Puritans quaintly put it. However, *some* suffering *can* be the result of a specific sin (for example, the man in John 5:1-15).

Sometimes the consequences of human sin can be more broadly distributed on the human scene in a way that does not appear very discriminating – such cases as war, plague, and congenital defects, for instance. Therefore, solely to use the categories of retribution and punishment to understand specific sins is quite hideous and insufficient.

The biblical writers have such a realistic estimation of both the human condition and the character of God that they, unlike us, are not so taken by surprise at human wickedness nor by the suffering it occasions. What is more, with such an understanding comes the overwhelming sense of the kindness of God as his blessings come to us all daily, but which we tend to take for granted (Matt. 5:45). This sense of amazement at such grace is reinforced by the fact that, in spite of our ingratitude and the way we treat each other, he still goes on being kind when perhaps we should expect more signs of his displeasure. We tend to reverse this perception, so that we expect that, without qualification, life should go along quite nicely for us. Accordingly we are often taken aback when trouble comes our way, sometimes issuing in resentment towards God. The biblical perspective, therefore, is a much-needed corrective in our hedonist-bound culture.

It is at this point that an objection is raised: 'If God does care about us and is so opposed to sin which is the cause of so much suffering in the world, why doesn't he intervene to do something about it?' Apart from this raising the question of the means and temporal conditions mentioned earlier, there are more sobering implications which we do not often think about but which have been well put by the writer, and no mean lay theologian, Dorothy L. Sayers:

> 'Why doesn't God smite this dictator dead?' is a question a little remote from us. Why, madam, did he not strike you dumb and imbecile before you uttered that baseless and unkind slander the day before yesterday? Or me, before I behaved with such a cruel lack of consideration to that well-meaning friend? And why sir, did he not cause your hand to rot off at the wrist before you signed your name to that dirty bit of financial trickery? You did not quite mean that? But why not? Your misdeeds and mine are none the less repellent because our opportunities for doing damage are less spectacular than those of some other people. Do you suggest that your doings and mine are too trivial for God to bother about? That cuts both ways; for in that case, it would make precious little difference to his creation if he wiped us both out tomorrow.[6]

In other words, if we want strict and immediate justice, then what we are asking for is literally hell, for that is precisely what it would be.

---

6. D. L. Sayers, 'The Triumph of Easter', *Creed or Chaos?* (Methuen, 1954).

However, in addition to looking backward for an answer to the question 'Why suffering?', one could also be looking forward so that what one is really asking is: 'What is the *purpose* of suffering? What possible good, if any, could there be in it?' This line of enquiry, too, is not without its prestigious proponents, for example, Irenaeus[7], Schleiermacher[8] and John Hick. This way of looking at the question was, in fact, taken up by a certain school of psychoanalysis called logotherapy, headed by Victor Frankle, who himself experienced the horrors of a Nazi concentration camp. It was there of all places that he noticed the positive way in which some people approached their situation. This observation in turn led him to quote Nietzsche with approval when he said that 'Men and women can endure any amount of suffering so long as they know the why to their existence'. In other words, if that suffering can be placed within some wider context of meaning and purpose, much, but by no means all, of the sting is taken out.

Although 'cause' and 'purpose' have here been distinguished as essentially providing two distinct approaches to the problem of pain, they are not

---

7. Irenaeus was Bishop of Lyons towards the middle of the second century. He wrote extensively against the heresy of Gnosticism in *Against Heresies* which also contains his thinking on the problem of evil.

8. Friedrich Schleiermacher (1768–1834) is often described as the 'Father of modern theology'. Although not consciously following Irenaeus, in his *The Christian Faith* he develops a type of theodicy remarkably similar.

mutually exclusive and have been brought together both philosophically and theologically. Philosophically they are drawn in to a unity by Aristotle and his idea of a 'final cause' – the end towards which something moves, its goal or *telos*. Theologically, both cause and purpose are embraced by the overarching doctrine of providence, of which the problem of evil is but one aspect. This is most clearly seen in Calvin's treatment of the subject, as when he writes:

> Although the paternal favour and beneficence, as well as the judicial severity of God, is often conspicuous in the whole course of his providence, yet occasionally as the causes of events are concealed, the thought is apt to rise, that human affairs are whirled about by blind Fortune. It is true, indeed, that if with sedate and quiet minds we were disposed to learn, the issue would at length make it manifest that the counsel of God is in accordance with the highest reason, that his purpose was either to train his people to patience, correct their depraved affections, tame their wantonness, inure them to self-denial; or on the other hand to cast down the proud, defeat the craftiness of the ungodly and frustrate all their schemes.[9]

Within Augustine's work also, purpose plays a major role as encapsulated in his now famous doctrine of

---

9. John Calvin, *Institutes of the Christian Religion*, 1:17 (Eerdmans, 1983).

O felix culpa (Blessed fault), such that 'God judged it better to bring good out of evil than to suffer no evil at all' (*Enchiridion*, XXVII). The redemption of sinners for Augustine is a far greater good than there being no sin at all.

PAIN WITH A PURPOSE?

There is a story in John 9 which illustrates the possibility of divine purpose in suffering: the healing of the man born blind. As Jesus and his disciples came across this man, it was the disciples who raised the question: 'Who sinned, this man or his parents?' They were looking for an answer to this tragic state of affairs in terms of causation linked to specific sinful action. But Jesus replied, 'Neither ... but this happened *so that* (Greek, *hina)* the work of God may be displayed in his life' (John 9:3). Jesus alters the perspective by focusing upon the divine purpose behind the situation, linking it to the creative-redeeming activity of God. Accordingly the man is healed.

This would appear to be where the theological centre of gravity lies in the New Testament, bearing in mind that the major concern of these writers is the practical one of enabling God's people to recognise that the suffering and persecution which they may be undergoing or are likely to face, when considered against the backcloth of God's eternal purpose, have creative significance. This comes out in several places, but as specific instances we may think of Romans 5:1-5, and later in 8:28ff.:

'And we know that in all things God works for the good of those who love him, who have been called according to his purpose' – a statement set within the context of Christian suffering.

But we may want to ask: 'Upon what grounds could Paul or anyone else make such a startling claim that God can and will work "all things to the good"?' This, in fact, brings us to the heart of the Christian faith, namely, the death and resurrection of Jesus Christ.

If a decisive insight into the mystery of suffering is to be found anywhere, then it is to be found at the cross where we come face to face with 'the God who is hidden in suffering' (Martin Luther). Here the foundational Christian belief is that the one who was known as Jesus of Nazareth was none other than the God who became man. He took to himself the sin of the world by bearing the penalty which is rightly ours; it involved absorbing evil, disarming principalities and powers, and reacting re-creatively to bring about the greater good. That is, it is seen as the means whereby people can be put in a right relationship with God; they are forgiven and receive eternal life (2 Cor. 5:19-21; 1 Pet. 2:24).

THE PERFECT PARADOX

It is at the cross that we are presented with the paradox running throughout the mysterious relationship between the evil of suffering and God's good purposes. From one point of view, the cross was the worst thing that could have happened (the murder of the divine Son, and so pinpointing even more forcefully our rebellious attitude towards God). Yet at the same time the cross was the best thing that ever happened (the divine means of rescuing us). Here we see God taking sin and suffering seriously because he tasted it first-hand in his Son, suffering physically and spiritually of a magnitude beyond our comprehension. It was this that shaped the New Testament writers' attitude towards suffering, by not only looking to Jesus as an example to follow (1 Pet. 3:17; Heb. 12:2), but as the theological centrepiece of the belief that the outworkings of what God has achieved by Jesus' death and resurrection in time will be brought to completion at the end of time, ushering in the new heaven and the new earth.

Wherever we look in the New Testament we cannot fail to be struck by the wonderful truth that the God whom we see in Jesus Christ is no remote God. He was not only willing to get his hands dirty, he was willing to get them pierced for the sake of those who did it, a point well made by Dorothy L. Sayers in her play, *The Man Born to be King*:

> For whatever reason God chose to make man as he is – limited and suffering and subject to sorrows and death – He had the honesty and the courage to take His own medicine. Whatever game He is playing with His creation He has kept his own rules and played fair. He has Himself gone through the whole of human

experience, from the trivial irritations of family life and lack of money to the worst horrors, pain, humiliation, defeat, despair and death. He was born in poverty and died in disgrace and felt it was all worthwhile.

Some of the good which can be brought out of evil can be glimpsed in this life. For example, through suffering we may become more caring, sympathetic and, in a profound way, more whole people. We are reminded, quite rightly, that we are not gods, but contingent beings. Also it is no bad thing to have our minds focused on eternal matters through pain, so coming to the realisation that this life is not the whole story. Suffering can be a means into a deeper, more intimate relationship with the God for whom we were made.

One person who has testified to this truth is Mary Craig who describes how two of her four sons were born with severe abnormalities, one with Hohler's syndrome and the other with Down's syndrome. Interestingly she speaks of 'redemptive suffering'. She writes:

In the teeth of the evidence I do not believe that any suffering is ultimately pointless or absurd, although it is often difficult to go on convincing oneself this. At first we react with incredulity, anger and despair. Yet the value of suffering does not lie in the pain of it but in what the sufferer makes of it. It is in sorrow that we discover the things that really matter; in sorrow that we discover ourselves.[10]

A similar perspective to that of Mary Craig was shared by the late Professor Sir Norman Anderson, whose son Hugh, after a brilliant career at Cambridge, died of cancer at the age of twenty-one. With the heavy heart of a bereaved father Professor Anderson wrote:

> People used continually to ask us why a young man of such promise, and with such a zest for life, should be allowed to die so young. To this the only reply, we both feel, is that we do not, cannot know. The vital question to ask God in such cases is not 'Why did you allow this?' (to which he seldom, I think, vouchsafes to answer), but 'What do you want to teach me through this?'[11]

How we respond is an important element in creating the right conditions for some good to be produced, but such a response requires a foundation. Both Mary Craig and Norman Anderson did not know the particular answer to the question 'Why?', but they did know why they trusted God who knew why, and that trust was based upon the solid foundation of God's revelation of himself in Jesus Christ.

---

10. Mary Craig, *Blessings,* (Hodder and Stoughton, 1979).
11. Norman Anderson, *An Adopted Son*, (IVP, 1985).

However, it is important to stress that not all good will be seen in this life, and here the eternal perspective is crucial.[12]

What is being suggested is that from the eternal perspective of God – the Author of the drama who 'sees the end from the beginning' – all creaturely decisions and responses are woven in with all other events to serve his purpose. The individual actions made do have significance in that they go towards making up patterns of lasting importance within the drama, but they do not exert an ultimate significance; that is provided by the Sovereign God who places the decisions and actions of his creatures into an eternal context which alone affords ultimate meaning.

An illustration which might give us some 'feel' of how this might be so is the well-known one of the weaving of Persian carpets. It is said that Persian carpets are made on a large frame. On one side of the frame stands the family placing threads into the framework, sometimes randomly, sometimes thoughtfully. On the other side of the frame stands the father, the master weaver, who takes all these threads and weaves them into a rich pattern of his design. When the carpet is completed the frame is then turned around for all to see.

---

12. This idea is developed in detail in V. P. White, *The Fall of a Sparrow* (Paternoster, 1985), and Melvin Tinker, *Purpose in Pain – Teleology and The Problem of Evil* (Themelios Vol. 16, No. 3, 1991).

With certain qualifications, God may be likened to the master weaver in this respect: that he takes each 'thread' (events and actions) and weaves them into a pattern which affords the 'threads' with significance. However, unlike the master weaver, God, from the beginning not only knows what those 'threads' are and where they will be placed on this side of the frame (a consequence of his omniscience), but he also decrees the events and actions themselves according to the eternal counsel of his will (a consequence of his omnipotence and wisdom). Some of the patterns and configurations can be discerned in this life (our side of the frame); however, it is only the other side of the frame (God's eternal purpose) which provides the lasting context in which ultimate significance is derived. The central point in that framework through which all of these threads are related and integrated is the life, death, resurrection, ascension and return of Jesus Christ.

THE ETERNAL PERSPECTIVE

Within our temporal context of experience some events are evil, including certain forms of suffering. But this is not the whole context, for another perspective is available. It is when the evil event is related to the wider context of God's eternal purposes that the evil is transfigured. Also it is within this broader God-given context that evil events can be seen to contain good *ends*. This does not take the evil out of evil, but it does mean that while evil is real, not illusion, its hold on reality is only temporary.

Let us focus how this might be so by thinking about the events surrounding the crucifixion. In terms of the betrayal, the trial, the scourging, the torture of the cross, the configuration of events is formed. Within this context such events are deemed evil, not least because man's wickedness is involved. But this is not the final, nor even the primary context from which these events derive their full significance (1 Cor. 2:7ff.); that is provided by God's action of redemption in which each event is a constituent part. I am not saying that the event of the cross is being transposed *into* something good by virtue of the resurrection, as if the resurrection is an effort at divine salvaging; rather, it is that the good (man's rescue from bondage to sin, the defeat of death, and so on) is already being wrought *in* and *through* the event of the cross itself, with the resurrection being but one vital aspect of the divine activity. The resurrection of Christ is also a revelation on our side of the frame, the significance of which is to be fully revealed at the end of time.

'If God is good and almighty, then why doesn't he do something about the fact of evil in general and suffering in particular?' The Christian's reply is that he has and he will. The goodness of God is maintained by relating each event to an intended good by placing it within the context of his own design, to be revealed at the end of time. The omnipotence of God is upheld by his weaving of all events into his eternal purpose, leaving nothing outside his ultimate control. Both the goodness and omnipotence of God in dealing with evil find their expression in a way that we could never have contemplated left to ourselves and that is in the cross of Christ.

THE GREATER GOOD DEFENCE

What has been presented is a form of what is called the Greater Good Defence,[13] which means that in some measure evil and suffering are justified by the greater good they occasion.

There is some force in the argument that for certain good ends to be achieved this logically entails certain evils. For example, the goods of compassion, sympathy and patience, logically and not simply contingently, require certain evils for them to be brought forth. This is the logical justification. However, it may be objected that such goods are outweighed by the evils that exist. In other words, that the evils endured are disproportionate to the goods produced, thus questioning the wisdom of introducing such evils in the first place. Thus an ethical justification is also required. Broadly speaking, such ethical justification takes two forms: non-punitive and punitive.

The non-punitive ethical justification is repre-sented by the Irenaean theodicy of Hick mentioned

---

13. See Paul Helm, *The Providence of God*, (IVP, 1993).

earlier ('theodicy' being the technical term used to describe the justification of the ways of God in the face of evil). He sees this world and the suffering within it as an occasion for 'soul making' which logically would not be possible in any other type of world (that is, one without suffering). However, for this to be a sufficient theodicy, it is necessary for Hick to postulate further worlds in which this soul-making process is continued, for it is evident that it does not benefit all in this world, for example, those who die young or unresponsively. It is also necessary for him to postulate universalism (all will be saved in the end) in order to counter the intuitive objection that without everyone achieving the beatific vision, God's good purpose is frustrated. However, both of these ideas find no basis in Scripture.

The punitive ethical justification is found in Augustine and Calvin. God may use an evil to punish a former evil. The use of Assyria by God to punish the sins of Israel, as we find in Isaiah 10, is an example of this. While there may be some measure of truth in this position (especially in that it takes God's justice seriously), it cannot constitute the *whole* of a theodicy. For one thing, it does not even begin to give a reason as to why God permitted evil in the first place, because for evil to punish evil presupposes the existence of evil which is to be punished! Also, as we have seen, not all suffering can be conceived solely within the framework of retribution.

Both theodicies have elements which go towards constituting a fully-orbed Christian theodicy. And it is in the cross of Christ that we see both elements displayed: pardon for sin and power for renewal, or justification and sanctification. One may also point out with Augustine, and his doctrine of *O felix culpa*, that not only is evil logically necessary for good to be wrought in us, but also for good to be expressed by *God* – for how could he show and we know and experience saving grace unless first of all there was something from which we needed saving?

NO SIMPLE SOLUTION

We have come full circle to the point where we began, namely, the relationship between evil, God's goodness and power. The scriptural testimony is that evil, sin and suffering are too deeply intertwined and all pervasive in the fabric of human existence to lend themselves to any simple solution. Furthermore, God's goodness embraces not only his undeserving love towards us but also his justice and his implacable opposition to all that is antithetical to his moral character. If it is simply justice we want, then that would mark the end of us all. If it is simply undeserved love or forgiveness we ask for, that would mark the end of a moral universe and God ceasing to be God. Simple justice God denies us; simple forgiveness God denies himself.

But what we see in the person and work of Jesus Christ on the cross is God's justice and God's love meeting in such a way that his omnipotence is paradoxically wrought in weakness. 'This is love,' says the apostle John, 'not that we loved God, but that he loved us and sent his Son as an atoning sacrifice for our sins' (1 John 4:10). And what that means is this: God's justice demands that sin (the root cause of all suffering in some way) is dealt with and punished. God's love is shown in that he took the punishment to himself in his Son on the cross, so that in the words of Barth, 'The Judge (Jesus) was judged in our place.' What we deserve (judgment and death), he willingly received, what we don't deserve (pardon and eternal life), he freely gives. What was achieved there, in veiled form and declared by the resurrection, will be declared before the whole of the universe at the end of time when the veil is finally lifted.

FOCUS ON THE CROSS

We end with a quote from P. T. Forsyth who, like Karl Barth after him, discovered the theological bankruptcy of the optimistic liberal theology upon which he had been raised, and turned instead to the deep theology of the Bible with the cross of Christ at the centre. In the midst of the carnage of the First World War, when optimistic self-reliant evolutionism was reaping its own rewards, he wrote his great *Justification of God*, in which he states:

> If the greatest act in the world, and the greatest crime there, became by the moral, holy victory of the Son of God, the source of not only endless

blessing to man, but perfect satisfaction and delight to a holy God, then there is no crime, no war, which is outside his control or impossible for his purpose. There is none that should destroy the Christian faith which has its object, source and sustenance in that cross and its victory, in which the prince of this world has in principle been judged and doomed for ever. In that cross we learn that faith which brings things not willed by God are yet worked up by God. In a divine irony, man's greatest crime turns God's greatest boon. The riddle is insoluble but the fact sure.[14]

14. P. T. Forsyth, *The Justification of God*, (Duckworth, 1916).

Chapter 2

What's Happening?

Job 1–3

In his biblically penetrating and pastorally helpful book, *How Long O Lord?*,[1] D. A. Carson relates the true story of a missionary who had been involved in very effective Christian work in Latin America. She was a woman full of love to the Lord Jesus and animated by a tremendous zeal for him. On returning home to the United States her future could not have looked more promising. Marrying a graduate of a Bible college, a man she had known for some years, she was set to return to the mission field with him.

But she had not been married to him for more than a few hours before she began to suspect that she had in fact married a monster. It soon transpired that he was an insecure bully who, while in public maintained a veneer of religious respectability, at home could only live with himself by demeaning everything his wife ever said or did. It began with a most malicious form

---

1.   D. A. Carson, *How Long, O Lord?* (IVP, 1990).

of psychological terror, later to develop into physical brutality. The mission board caught on pretty quickly and refused to send them out.

As the years passed the abuse worsened. The woman tried talking to friends and counsellors; some of whom simply sided with the husband and told her to try harder. Eventually she turned to drink and a couple of years later she was a confirmed alcoholic, finding herself becoming brutal with her two children. She hated herself, she hated her husband, and she hated God. Her cry, quite understandably, was, 'Why me, Lord?' After all, she had done nothing to deserve this. She knew that she was not perfect, but she had been such a devoted Christian. So what possible reason could there be for her to be cast into such a living hell? It simply did not make sense.

We have to admit that such suffering does not make sense. We can see a connection between certain forms of behaviour and the suffering they occasion, for example, sexual promiscuity and venereal disease. But what possible connection could there be in terms of desert to account for the appalling atrocities undergone by the Jews during the Holocaust? As we contemplate the holocaust in all its naked evil, can we honestly believe that all those children tortured by the Nazis were not in a very real sense *innocent sufferers*?

There is one book in the Bible which perhaps more than any other wrestles with the problem of innocent suffering and that is the book of Job. It is in these pages that with remarkable candour its writer raises the perplexing question which is on the lips of so many: Why do bad things happen to good people?

STEPPING INTO JOB'S SHOES

If we are to allow the full emotive import of this poetic *magnum opus* to have its effect on us, we must try putting ourselves into Job's shoes, to empathise with the very real, heartfelt cries that his unjust suffering evokes.

In the book's first two chapters we are introduced to Job. He lives at a time when a person's wealth is measured not in terms of the size of his bank balance but the size of his herds. This would place him in the period of the Hebrew patriarchs, men like Abraham, Isaac and Jacob. Job is not only a wealthy man, indeed possibly *the* wealthiest man alive according to verse 3, but he is also a godly man. We are told that he feared God and shunned evil. His deep personal piety showed itself in several ways, not least in his passionate concern for the spiritual well-being of his children. In verses 4-5 we read that in case his sons and daughters had behaved in a way that might have offended God and brought down his judgement upon them, Job went out of his way to make sacrifices for their sin on their behalf. And this was no passing fad for Job – we are told that this was his regular custom:

His sons used to take turns holding feasts in their homes, and they would invite their three sisters to eat and drink with them. When a period of feasting had run its course, Job would send and have them purified. Early in the morning he would sacrifice a burnt offering for each of them, thinking, 'Perhaps my children have sinned and cursed God in their hearts.' This *was Job's regular custom (1:4-5)*.

Today we would describe Job as a committed Christian, one whose faith penetrated every area of his life.

In order to pre-empt any cynical doubt which may be in our minds that all of this wealth has been gained by shady double-dealing, it is made quite clear from the outset that Job was 'blameless and upright' (1:8); in other words, his moral character was impeccable. So, here we have a sincere worshipper of God, an honest, hard-working businessman, a loving husband and thoughtful father who is second to none; in fact Job almost appears to be too good to be true. But as we shall see, Job was one of those rare individuals who exist within a class all by themselves, he was a genuinely good man. Therefore what could possibly go wrong?

Job has done nothing which would require any change in lifestyle. His relationship with God could hardly have been better. There are no obvious lessons he has to learn or sins which need correcting and it is very difficult to see how he could improve significantly. 'Surely,' some would argue, 'being faithful to God brings with it its own rewards – a good and peaceful life, doesn't it?'

BEHIND THE SCENES

In 1:6 the curtains of visible reality are lifted for a moment to provide the readers with a glimpse into the invisible spirit world where, behind the scenes, a wager is being made between God and the devil, Satan, whose very name means 'accuser of God's people'. Like a vindictive lawyer or a corrupt policeman with an obsession to frame the innocent, Satan was on the look-out for someone to drag before the judgement seat of God in order to condemn.

When God said to Satan, 'Where have you come from?' Satan answered, 'From roaming through the earth and going to and fro in it.' When God asked Satan, 'Have you thought about my servant Job? There is no one like him. He is quite blameless and morally upright', Satan, in effect, replied: 'The only reason why Job behaves as he does is because he knows on which side his bread is buttered. He is religious and moral only because of what he can get out of it. After all, everyone knows that religion is nothing but enlightened self-interest. Believe in God, be a good boy and up you go to heaven! Be a naughty boy and a pagan and it's a deep fry for you down below. It's just a matter of the right carrot and stick with Job. In fact, you can put it all down to his rather fortunate circumstances which you have provided, God. Anybody can afford to be religious when they have a lifestyle like that. Religion is nothing but a luxury for the idle rich, the upper-middle classes. But let Job have a taste of what real need is and you will soon see where his true love lies.' That has been the taunt of Satan regarding countless people down the ages.

Accordingly, Satan challenges God: 'Stretch out your hand and strike everything he has, and he will surely curse you to your face' (verse 11). And shocking though it may seem, God takes up the challenge and actually gives Satan permission to do his worst, with one proviso – he is not to harm Job himself: 'The LORD said to Satan, "Very well, then, everything he has is in your hands, but on the man himself do not lay a finger"' (vv. 11-12).

A WORLD FALLS APART

That is precisely what happened. In what has all the ingredients of a screaming nightmare, Job's life was totally devastated. First, he lost his wealth to marauding bandits. Gone are his oxen needed for farming, gone are his donkeys and camels needed for transport, and all his workers are massacred (vv. 14-15). His financial empire lies in ruins. And just as he may have been consoling himself with the thought that bad as that is, he could just manage to scrape a living together with the few sheep he had left, news reached him that these too had been destroyed, not by an act of man this time but by an act of God: 'The fire of God fell from the sky and burned up the sheep and the servants' (v. 16). Maybe it was a volcanic eruption. While still reeling from the shock waves of economic catastrophe, news of an even greater personal tragedy comes to his ears – a storm has taken the lives of his dear children (vv. 18-19).

How would we have responded to all of that? This was Job's response:

> At this, Job got up and tore his robe and shaved his head [signs of intense grief and mourning]. Then he fell to the ground in worship and said: 'Naked I came from my mother's womb, and naked I shall depart. The LORD gave and the LORD has taken away; may the name of the LORD be praised.'

Then we read: 'In all this, Job did not sin by charging God with wrongdoing' (vv. 20-22).

ENOUGH IS ENOUGH?

We may think that that would be enough for any man to bear. But God apparently thought differently. For, as the veil is lifted once more in chapter 2, we find ourselves in the heavenly court yet again, only to discover the wager being taken one stage further. Satan, still not convinced that there is not a base ulterior motive for Job's faith, pursues his challenge in verses 4-5: 'Skin for skin! A man will give all he has for his own life. But stretch out your hand and strike his flesh and bones and he will surely curse you to your face.' In other words, 'Get under Job's skin, God, let him feel some physical suffering, let him think that his own life is threatened, and then watch him reveal his true colours.'

So Job was afflicted with boils of such excruciating pain that his wife, finding it unbearable to watch, urged Job to commit voluntary euthanasia by cursing God (verse 9). Why, even Job himself wishes that he had never been born, which is the cry at the centre of 3:11f.:

> Why did I not perish at birth,
>   and die as I came from the womb?
> Why were there knees to receive me
>   and breasts that I might be nursed?
> For now I would be lying down in peace;
>   I would be asleep and at rest
> with kings and counsellors of the earth,
>   who built for themselves places now lying in ruins,
> with rulers who had gold,
>   who filled their houses with silver.

So disfigured and ruined was Job that when his friends Eliphaz, Bildad and Zophar arrived to console him, they hardly recognised him and broke down in uncontrollable weeping, it was that bad (2:11-13). This was a man undergoing suffering alright, a suffering which was heightened, not lessened, by his faith in God. For if he had not believed in God it would have been some cold comfort to know that it was all a result of chance, with no-one to blame. But to believe in God, and a good and all powerful God at that, seemed to fly in the face of his present experience. How could such a God allow this to happen?

In these opening chapters of the book of Job, there are three lessons which the writer is insistent we learn if we are going to make any progress in coping with the problem of the suffering of the innocent.

WHO IS IN CHARGE?

The first lesson is that God is sovereign over suffering: that in a mysterious way which we cannot fathom, suffering falls within his overruling power.

One of the ways some people try to resolve the problem of evil is to become what are called *dualists*. This idea suggests that there are two equal and opposite forces battling it out in the world – good and evil, God and Satan. All the good that happens is due to God and all the bad is due to Satan. The result is that God bears no responsibility when it comes to suffering because it's not really his fault. The blame belongs to Satan. In philosophical form this view is represented by the ancient religion of Zoroastrianism and in popular form by 'Star Wars'. But some Christians have imbibed it too.

A few years ago I visited a Christian fellowship which had really gone overboard with this type of thinking. One member stood up and said he had lost his car keys and that this was an attack by Satan. Another said that he had noisy next-door neighbours, and this too was an attack by Satan. Another had a verruca and this, as well, could be put down to Satan. These people couldn't have a cold without it being turned into a major spiritual battle!

Such a notion may be convenient and simple, but the theological price is very high. In this idea we are left with a God who is limited, a God who is absolutely dependent upon the moves of his opponent Satan. Perhaps, one day, he may even be outwitted by Satan and then where would we be? The Bible, however, and especially the book of Job, will not allow us to believe that sort of nonsense.

Instead, we are presented with a God who is absolutely sovereign, in total control. Although Satan is involved, he is not presented as a second god but as a creature with remarkable powers, who is able to use these powers only by divine permission. Certainly, Job's troubles can be attributed to the activity of Satan, as they can *also* be attributed to the activity of the robbers and viruses. This is called dual causality or a concursive understanding. None of these things could have happened had God not *permitted* them to happen. In Job 1:11 Satan challenged God to stretch out his hand against Job. But it is God who put the power into Satan's hands! Job too recognised the sovereignty of God, for example in 2:10, when he said to his wife: 'Shall we accept good from God, and not trouble?'

From one point of view, knowing this simply makes matters worse, because it presses us to plead the question 'Why?' Why should a good God decree or allow such things if he has the power to stop them? But from another point of view it provides us with hope. Because if God is good (and he is) then we can believe that there is some good reason behind what happens, *even* though it may not be known to us at the time. What is more, if he is all powerful (and he is), then there is hope that he has the power to relieve our sufferings or at least provide us with the grace to cope. The message coming over loud and clear is that it is God, and not the devil, who rules.

SPEAK OUT

The second lesson we need to learn from this introduction is that God does not blame us if, in our suffering, we vent our feelings to him, that we cry to him, or even shout at him if necessary, so unloading the emotional pain on to him. That is what Job does in chapter 3.

After the relatively passive reaction to the news of his children's death – which is often the case in bereavement, a numbness and disbelief which is part of the body's natural mechanism for coping – there follows his deep emotional outburst. While not sinning by cursing God, Job does not hesitate to curse the day he was born. So anguished is he that he feels he must tell someone, and who better to tell than God? And it is vital that people who are undergoing pain do not bottle up their feelings, for if that happens all the energy simply gets pushed down into the subconscious, only to show itself later, either in depression or in a nervous stress. Far better to let the grief come out. That is why I always stress to someone who has recently been bereaved that at the funeral service it is right to show how one feels – it is OK to cry. There is no virtue in the British stiff upper lip; it is not true to say, 'Didn't she cope well at the funeral?' because she showed no emotion. That is not coping, it is denying. We all need to have permission to grieve so that we can move towards some sort of recovery. God respects that, indeed he approves of it. As we shall see in the following chapters, God did not rebuke Job for expressing his doubts or anger.

Many know the story of the Christian writer C. S. Lewis who married Joy Davidman, as depicted in the film *Shadowlands*. Joy Davidman eventually died a painful death by cancer, leaving behind two young boys. In a very candid account, Lewis wrote down his feelings after his wife had died which we read in his book *A Grief Observed*.[2] Like Job, Lewis faces up to his agony and argues with himself and God about how he feels. He writes:

> Tonight all the hells of young grief have opened again; the mad words, the bitter resentment, the fluttering in the stomach, the nightmare unreality, the wallowed-in-tears. Meanwhile where is God? This is one of the most disquieting symptoms. When you are happy ... and turn to him in gratitude and praise, you will be welcomed – so it feels – with open arms. But go to him when your need is desperate, when all other help is vain, and what do you find? A door slammed in your face, and a sound of bolting and double bolting on the inside. After that, silence.

---

2.   C. S. Lewis, *A Grief Observed* (Fount, 1962).

That is a very honest expression of his experience. And we might well remember someone else who expressed similar sentiments from a cross, when he cried: 'My God, my God, why have you forsaken me?' We can and must express our anguish.

MASTERING THE MYSTERY

Finally, we must still continue to realise that there is an irreducible element of mystery. Job cried out: 'Why?'; 'Why didn't I perish at birth?'; 'Why was I not stillborn?'; 'Why is light given to those in misery?' And Job was never given the answers. Although we as readers are allowed to have insight into what is going on in heaven, Job is not. He is never made aware of the discussion between God and Satan. That is important, because one of the lessons this biblical book is teaching is the need to trust God in situations when we do not know why certain things are happening. But let it be said that this faith is not blind faith. Job knew about God, he had reasons to believe that God is all powerful and all good, and he is reminded of these things later when he encounters God as described in chapters 38–42. Therefore, although Job did not know why these things were happening to him, he did know enough about God to know why he trusted him who did know why. The fact that Job didn't get an answer didn't stop him from asking, and neither should it stop us.

What Job was experiencing was an inscrutable mystery, nevertheless he kept on trusting.

We have to admit that if we can see that there is a good outcome to suffering it helps us to endure it better – like a woman going through childbirth, for instance. In the Christian life, however, we are not always permitted to know the reason why. But we are still called to trust God who knows why. Let me give you an actual example.

In a small town in Australia, there was a Christian woman who was crippled with arthritis, her body was more or less continually racked with pain. One neighbour who lived a few houses down the street knew this, and was struck by the gracious way she coped with it, never complaining, always being positive. This impressed her so much that she decided to go to the woman's church to find out more about a belief which could make such a difference to a life. Eventually she became a Christian. She then began to take her young son along to church, and he also became a Christian. Today, that son is one of the finest New Testament scholars in the world and a model Christian man. I am sure that if we had been able to say to that woman, 'Keep on, put up with your suffering because it is going to be such a witness that a young boy is going to be converted through it, and he is going to be greatly used by God to influence thousands of ministers throughout the world,' then that would undoubtedly have made her suffering easier to bear. But she didn't know any of that. All she could do was to trust God.

All that Job could do, and maybe all that we can do too, in the face of the unanswerable, is to trust in the God whom we know has tasted suffering first-hand in his beloved Son, Jesus Christ.

Chapter 3

'With Friends Like These …'

Job 4–31

Several years ago the French atheist, Jean Paul Sartre, wrote a play entitled *The Devil and the Good Lord*. The main character in the drama is Goetz, a butchering soldier who gives up his murderous ways to become a Christian, indeed, almost a saint. As the play progresses Goetz gradually becomes disillusioned with what he considers to be God's silence. He prays but gets no answer. He finally bursts out: 'I prayed, I demanded a sign. I sent messages to heaven, no reply. Heaven ignored my very name. Each minute I wonder what I could *be* in the eyes of God. Now I know the answer: nothing. God does not see me, God does not hear me, God does not know me. You see this emptiness over our heads? That is God. You see this gap in the door? It is God. You see that hole in the ground? That is God again. Silence is God. Absence is God. God is the loneliness of man.'

About fifty years earlier Joseph Parker, a Christian preacher who was minister of the City Temple in London, said that up to the age of sixty-eight he had never had a religious doubt, but then his wife died and his faith all but collapsed. He wrote: 'In that dark hour, I became almost an atheist. For God had set his foot upon my prayers and treated my petitions with contempt. If I had seen a dog in such agony as mine, I would have pitied and helped the dumb beast; yet God spat upon me and cast me out as an offence – out into the waste wilderness and the night black and starless.'[1]

Just where is God when your world is falling apart? Why doesn't he *say* something? Why does he not *do* something, even if it is simply putting an end to the misery by taking away our life? Those are the cries of men like Sartre and Parker, and they may have been your cries too. They were certainly the heartfelt yearnings of Job.

Job, the model of godliness, the paradigm of virtue, kindness itself, is now reduced to a pitiful, whimpering wreck. His livelihood is in ruins, his family is dead and his health all but broken. In fact, he has very little left save two things: his faith – just, and his integrity. In the central sections of the book, which we are considering in this chapter, both of these come under a blistering attack from, would you believe, three of his closest friends. And we may well think that with friends like these who needs enemies!

---

1. Quoted by John Stott in *The Cross of Christ*, p. 312 (IVP, 1986).

Two positions

No matter how crass, misleading and insensitive Job's three counsellors – Eliphaz, Bildad and Zophar – proved to be, however, there is no doubt that their intentions were good and sincere. In their own way they represent a certain type of Christian which is to be found today. If we wanted to summarise their position it would be: 'Don't confuse me with the facts, my mind is made up.' Even before Job opens his mouth they have already decided what the real problem is and where the problem lies. The problem is sin and it lies with Job. It can't be God's fault, they think – he wouldn't do such a thing without a reason, and the *only* reason they could see for God inflicting such suffering is in judgement. Judgement upon what? Well, upon Job's sin, of course!

On the other hand, we have Job who also in his own way represents a certain group of Christians; and if we were to sum up his position it could be in the words of a John Lennon song: 'Gimme some truth.' In effect Job is saying to his friends: 'I don't want your theories, however logical and convincing they may be to you. I want to get to the bottom of what is really going on. I want the truth. More than that I want to meet the truth – God himself, so that he can vindicate me and declare me innocent before the world. To suffer physical pain and loss is one thing, but to suffer false accusations of being a liar, a cheat and deserving what is happening, as my friends are saying, is one pain too many, and only God can put it right.' That is the burden of these chapters.

The way the drama is set out is as follows. Each of Job's friends in turn attack him verbally. After each assault Job defends himself. This cycle of attack, defence and counter attack is repeated three times, until eventually Job explodes in one long outburst reducing his friends to silence. Even so, he still does not succeed in convincing them that he is innocent. Their minds were made up and they didn't want to be confused by the facts.

JOB, IT'S YOUR FAULT!

Their reasoning was quite simple and went something like this: all suffering is due to wickedness. Job is suffering, therefore he is wicked. What could be simpler? We see this in Eliphaz's speech in 4:7-9:

> 'Consider now: Who, being innocent, has ever perished?
>   Where were the upright ever destroyed?
> As I have observed, those who plough evil
>   and those who sow trouble reap it.
> At the breath of God they are destroyed;
>   at the blast of his anger they perish.'

Eliphaz prides himself in being an astute observer of human affairs, a proper little sociologist cum theologian is Eliphaz. 'Everyone knows, Job, that God has ordered the world in terms of moral cause and effect. If you are good you prosper, if you are bad, then eventually your sins will find you out. You can't escape it, any more than you can escape the law of gravity; it's immutable.'

What is more, Eliphaz claims that he has had a special revelation confirming this – a vision, what some today would claim to be 'a word from the Lord'. And who can argue against that?

> 'A word was secretly brought to me,
>   my ears caught a whisper of it.
> Amid disquieting dreams in the night,
>   when deep sleep falls on men,
> fear and trembling seized me
>   and made all my bones shake.
> A spirit glided past my face,
>   and the hair on my body stood on end.
> It stopped,
>   but I could not tell what it was.
> A form stood before my eyes,
>   and I heard a hushed voice:
> "Can a mortal be more righteous than God?
>   Can a man be more pure than his Maker?"'(4:12-17)

The implication is obvious, 'You suffer, Job, because you have sinned.'

But, not only do these friends have sociology and the charismatic movement on their side, they have the whole weight of church tradition too, so says Bildad in chapter 8:2-3, 8-10.

> 'How long will you say such things?
>   Your words are a blustering wind.
> Does God pervert justice?
>   Does the Almighty pervert what is right?'

> 'Ask the former generations
>   and find out what their fathers learned,
> for we were born only yesterday and know nothing,

> and our days on earth are but a shadow.
> Will they not instruct you and tell you?
> Will they not bring forth words from their understanding?'

That is, 'This is no novel idea, Job, that God operates according to strict justice. As you well know, it is the received wisdom of our elders, men far wiser than you have come to this conclusion. So why don't you stop being so obstinate? Admit your sin and repent. Nothing could be simpler.'

Job, however, remains unmoved. No matter how sound and orthodox their ideas are, and Job admits they are (9:1), the theory does not tie in with his experience, it does not do justice to the facts. Certainly, it is a rule of thumb that what a man sows, so shall he reap – live a loose life and end up a drug addict or an alcoholic. That at least makes some sense. But that is not Job's situation and it is wrong to pretend otherwise.

Eventually, after listening to Job's special pleading, which in itself may have confirmed his guilt in his friends' eyes – he protests *too* much – the third of his friends, Zophar, can't stomach any more. He knows what he believes and he is sticking with it and, no matter how pathetic and unkind his words may be, he is going to give Job a piece of his mind.

> 'Are all these words to go unanswered?
> Is this talker to be vindicated?
> Will your idle talk reduce men to silence?
> Will no-one rebuke you when you mock?

You say to God, "My beliefs are flawless
>   and I am pure in your sight."
Oh, how I wish that God would speak,
>   that he would open his lips against you
and disclose to you the secrets of wisdom,
>   for true wisdom has two sides.
Know this: God has even forgotten some of your sin'
>   (11:2-6).

In a torrent of rage, Zophar and his two colleagues are practically bullying Job into signing a false confession. 'Look,' he is saying, 'you may be able to fool some people with this "Butter wouldn't melt in my mouth" story. But you don't fool God. If he were here he would soon put you in your place. Why, so great is your sin, so long is the list of them that even God couldn't keep a complete record, that's why he's forgotten some of them.'

Later, in 22:4-11 Eliphaz is even more mercilessly brutal in coming to the point:

'Is it for your piety that he rebukes you
>   and brings charges against you?
Is not your wickedness great?
>   Are not your sins endless?
You demanded security from your brothers for no reason;
>   you stripped men of their clothing, leaving them naked.
You gave no water to the weary
>   and you withheld food from the hungry,
though you were a powerful man, owning land –
>   an honoured man, living on it.
And you sent widows away empty-handed
>   and broke the strength of the fatherless.
That is why snares are all around you,

> why sudden peril terrifies you,
> why it is so dark that you cannot see,
> and why a flood of water covers you.'

In other words, 'Everyone knows how rich men get their wealth – double dealing on the side, fiddling the books, exploiting the poor. So that's how you must have come upon your wealth, Job, and God has found you out and is giving you your just deserts.' The solution each of them gives to Job is the same: repent, come clean and turn to God and you will soon be restored to your former prosperity. For example in 22:21: 'Submit to God and be at peace with him; in this way prosperity will come to you.'

NEAT BUT NARROW THEOLOGY

Their theology was all very neat and tidy, admitting of no loose ends. It explained things remarkably well, so well in fact they didn't have to bother thinking for themselves, it was all done for them in their theory of retribution. So what if some of the facts didn't seem to fit? They could either be conveniently ignored or forced to fit. But it is just a little too convenient. These people would have queried the title of this book, for according to their thinking (and the thinking of some today), bad things don't happen to good people, only to bad people.

As we saw in our opening chapter, the Bible does teach that *some* suffering is punishment for sin, but not *all* suffering is to be viewed in this way. What Job's friends were doing was mistaking part of the truth for the whole truth. But the result was appalling. They add more suffering to one who is already at breaking point by trying to get him to abandon one of the few things left which is precious to him, his integrity. By this verbal arm twisting they aim to get him to say that which he does not believe to be true. But they also blind themselves, foreclosing on any possibility that their understanding might be broadened. Because everything is cut and dried they do not consider any other possibility, in particular that it might be they rather than Job who are wrong. That possibility never crosses their minds.

Here there is a warning for us all, namely, however sincere, we must be careful not to become a Job's comforter. To begin with, it is obvious that they really didn't hear what Job was saying. Oh, they let him speak, they heard out his objections, but they gave them no real consideration whatsoever. And that hurts. When you are going through a crisis, deep emotional pain, then the last thing you want is for your own integrity to be violated, for someone to treat you as if you are less than a human being, without thoughts, without feelings – but just an object to be assailed with 'the right answers'. It seems that whatever concerns these friends had for Job, those concerns were overridden by a greater concern, namely, the concern to keep their own watertight beliefs intact. It was far more important to them that they should not allow their ideas to be brought into question than for truth to be pursued however uncomfortable that might be. It is sad that Christians are not immune to this rather unfortunate habit of burying their heads in the sand instead of rigorously thinking something through.

What is perhaps worse is the cruelty of adding to a person's pain guilt which doesn't really belong to him. A modern day example of this is the increasingly popular 'healing prosperity' or 'name it and claim it teaching'. The teaching goes something like this: if you have an illness, have faith and you will be healed. If you are not healed it is because you haven't got enough faith, or because your wife doesn't have enough faith, or because your great-uncle was a Freemason! Is this an exaggeration? Here is an account written by a notable Christian physician of a healing crusade at Horsforth in Leeds several years ago:

> One night a friend of mine who is deaf in one ear thought he would have a go at being healed. Hands were laid upon him and he was told that he was healed, but he said, 'I am not.' The healer said, 'Yes, you are.' 'No, I am not,' my friend insisted, only to be told, 'Well, it must be that you have not got sufficient faith.' After a brief altercation the healer went on down the line of deaf people. When the healing activities had finished my friend turned to the lady next to him and said, 'What did he do for you, love?'

and she replied with her hand cupped to her ear, 'What did you say?'[2]

This is a theology with no loose ends, which does not admit innocent suffering, which adds pain upon pain.

INTEGRITY MATTERS

Job will have none of it. Whatever the majority might say, however impeccable the orthodoxy of his friends or whatever alleged special revelations they have received, he knows the truth and will not sacrifice his integrity on the altar of neat popular thinking. Although, like an innocent man after prolonged interrogation by his captors, it must have been so tempting to give up and take the easy way out, and say, 'OK, I'm guilty, just let me out of this hell', Job had the courage to say 'No'. Whatever is going on, it is not his fault and he will not be brutalised into false humility by taking the rap for something he did not do:

> 'As surely as God lives, who has denied me justice,
>> the Almighty, who has made me taste bitterness of soul,
> as long as I have life within me,
>> the breath of God in my nostrils,
> my lips will not speak wickedness,
>> and my tongue will utter no deceit.
> I will never admit you are in the right;
>> till I die, I will not deny my integrity.

---

2. Prof. Verna Wright, 'A medical view of miraculous healing', in *Sword and Trowel*, 1987, No 1.

I will maintain my righteousness and never let go of it;
my conscience will not reproach me as long as I live'
(27:2-5).

In vain Job tries to demonstrate to his friends that it is they who have got it wrong. They held two beliefs. The first was that all wicked suffer. The second was that all who suffer are wicked. And both of these propositions are patently false, says Job. In chapter 21 he points out that many a tyrant has lived the life of Riley only to die peacefully in his bed. It is simply not true to say that the wicked don't get away with it, for it is patently obvious they do. This has always been the case, with a few notable exceptions. Ask the pimps and the drug pushers whether crime does not pay, and they will look at you as if you are mad. Of course it pays, and they will point to the Daimlers and plush homes to prove the point. What is more, says Job, it is not true to say that all who suffer are wicked, look at me!

In chapters 29–31 Job gives a most moving recital of all the godly things he did before his world fell apart. He had been honest, disciplined, rescued the poor, helped the blind, comforted those who mourned, and made a promise not to look lustfully at a girl. He opened his home to countless strangers, he never rejoiced over their misfortune saying 'Serves them right', and he never trusted in his own wealth. All very reminiscent of someone else who was falsely accused. 'He must be wicked,' cried the crowd on Good Friday, 'for only the wicked get crucified. The Bible says so in Deuteronomy 21:22-23. He saved others, let him save himself.' Those were the cold words of Jesus' comforters. Although he didn't know it, Job was in very good company indeed, the company of the Son of God himself.

ONLY GOD WILL DO

What Job wanted was not some theoretical problem-solving of the 'Why does God allow evil?' variety, which philosophers and sceptics are so adept at asking. He wanted to meet with God. He wanted to hear *God's* voice, to hear God's reason for allowing this appalling act of human misery:

> 'I loathe my very life;
>   therefore I will give free rein to my complaint
> and speak out in the bitterness of my soul.
>   I will say to God: Do not condemn me,
> but tell me what charges you have against me.
>   Does it please you to oppress me,
> to spurn the work of your hands,
>   while you smile on the schemes of the wicked?'
>   (10:1-3)

Job turns to God to plead with him to show himself just for once and explain this injustice, for that is what Job is convinced it is, an act of injustice perpetrated by God, and that is the thing that hurts most of all. In a fit of deep depression he longs for the days when he knew God's kindness:

'How I long for the months gone by,
    for the days when God watched over me,
when his lamp shone upon my head
    and by his light I walked through darkness!
Oh, for the days when I was in my prime,
    when God's intimate friendship blessed my house,
when the Almighty was still with me
    and my children were around me,
when my path was drenched with cream
    and the rock poured out for me streams of olive oil'
                                    (29:1-5).

Isn't that moving? He wants to be with God.

The amazing thing is this: although Job sails very close to the wind, and borders on blasphemy, he never ceases to believe. Not once does he slip over into atheism – he simply can't:

'Though he slay me, yet will I hope in him;
    I will surely defend my ways to his face.
Indeed, this will turn out for my deliverance,
    for no godless man would dare come before him!'(13:15-16).

He is so convinced of his innocence that he is willing to die if that is the only way he can come before God to vindicate himself for he is sure God will clear his name. But it is *God* he wants. Yes, he wants an explanation. Yes, he wants his name cleared. But most of all he wants God. And, as we shall see in the next chapter, his heart's desire was eventually granted, but not until many more tears were shed.

Like Job, we too are to be content with none other than a true personal knowledge of God. Don't be content with theories about him, or clever ideas about the problem of evil – settle for nothing less than God himself, however many tears have to be cried in the process.

But where is God to be found? Of all places, on a cross. If we really want to know what God is like and to have that intimacy of fellowship with him, then that is where we begin to look, at the God-man Jesus, who also knew the dark cloud of suffering, the rejection and misunderstanding, and who, having gone through it all, now rules this broken world of ours. In the words of the writer to the Hebrews, who sought to encourage young believers whose faith was being sorely tested like Job's: 'We see Jesus, who was made a little lower than the angels, now crowned with glory and honour because he suffered death, so that by the grace of God he might taste death for everyone' (2:9). It is at the cross we find God.

Chapter 4

GOD HAS SPOKEN

Job 32–41

In 1944 a fourteen-year-old Hungarian Jewish boy named Elie Wiesel was taken with his mother and sister by the Gestapo and herded into a cattle wagon crammed with eighty other people. For three days they travelled like this until they arrived at Auschwitz concentration camp. The men and women were segregated and Elie never saw his mother or sister again. He wrote: 'Never shall I forget that night, the first night in camp, which has turned my life into one long night, seven times cursed and seven times sealed. Never shall I forget that smoke (of the crematorium) ... never shall I forget those flames which consumed my faith for ever.... Never shall I forget those moments which murdered my God and my soul and turned my dreams to dust. Some talked of God, of his mysterious ways, of the sins of the Jewish people, and of their future deliverance. But I had ceased to pray. How I sympathised with Job! I did not deny God's existence, but I doubted his absolute justice.'[1]

---

1. Elie Wiesel, *Night* (Penguin, 1981).

A DEADLY DILEMMA

It has long been recognised that the existence of suffering in the world has posed a problem for the believer in God, especially the Christian. It is sometimes put in the form of the dilemma we examined at the beginning of this book: If God is perfectly loving he must wish to abolish evil. If God is all powerful he must be able to abolish evil. But evil exists, therefore God cannot be both all good and all powerful. How do we respond to that?

As we have seen there are several simple solutions to the problem which in some way or other involve denying one of those beliefs which make up the dilemma in the first place. So some people would deny that God is all powerful. I remember attending a clergy conference where a deaconess believed in what she called 'a weak God' and she was adamant that it gave her comfort to think that God was busy struggling with life like the rest of us. On the other hand, some would deny the existence of evil, like the sect Christian Science which puts it all down to an illusion of the mind. But then again, there would be others who would want to question God's goodness, especially his justice. That is what Elie Wiesel was doing, and that too was what Job found himself doing. He knew that God was all powerful. He certainly knew that suffering was real, only too real. But as we saw in the last chapter, in his mind his predicament did bring into question God's goodness. In verse 1 of chapter 27 he explicitly states that God has denied him justice.

What was it that drove Job to this conclusion? Job the philanthropist, Job the 'Christian' who even in his darkest moments refused to curse God. So why this astounding claim that God is not just? The answer would appear to be that Job too had bought into the theory of retributive justice. He also seemed to share with his friends the view that it is through suffering that God executes his judgement in the world. But where he *disagreed* with them was in their conclusion that he must be suffering because of *his* sin. Therefore, given the theory that all suffering is God's judgement, the only conclusion Job can come to is that God is not exercising his judgement fairly. He knows that he is the innocent one and so it must be that God is the guilty one.

However, there are two further encounters which correct both Job and his three friends and open up the way for a different understanding of why God allows suffering. The first encounter is with another, much younger, counsellor, Elihu, who until now has remained silent. The second is an encounter with God himself.

A YOUNG TURK

When we come across Elihu in chapter 32, he is obviously a very angry young man. He has not spoken because he feels that as a younger person it is both wise and respectful to allow his elders to have their say first: 'I am young in years and you are old, that is why I was fearful, not daring to tell you what I know' (v. 6). But eventually he comes to the point where he can hold in his anger no longer. He has listened to the three counsellors and he has listened to Job, and he finds them all to be totally unconvincing. The three friends have simply not answered Job's objections, as Elihu points out in verse 12. Job has run rings around them until eventually they give up trying to argue, being reduced to adopting the 'we are right and you are wrong and that's all there is to it' attitude. But Job too has incensed Elihu, not because of his protested innocence, Elihu believes him on that score, but because he is so eager to clear his own reputation at the expense of God's reputation:

> 'But you have said in my hearing –
>> I heard the very words –
> "I am pure and without sin;
>> I am clean and free from guilt.
> Yet God has found fault with me;
>> he considers me his enemy.
> He fastens my feet in shackles;
>> he keeps close watch on all my paths."
> But I tell you, in this you are not right,
>> for God is greater than man' (33:8-12).

Then again in 34:12 we read: 'It is unthinkable that God would do wrong, that the Almighty would pervert justice.' 'Look,' he in effect is saying to Job, 'you may well be as innocent as you say, and it will not do for your three friends to bring that into question; but by the same token it will not do for you to question God's innocence. You may not have sinned so grossly when you started but you are coming pretty close to it now. You are wrong.'

The first reason why Elihu rightly believes Job to be wrong is because 'God is greater than man' (33:12). Not simply that he is more powerful, but that his plans and purposes are on such a grand scale, far more complex and involved than our tiny minds can ever fully fathom. In the words of Isaiah 55:9, his ways are not our ways and his thoughts are higher than our thoughts. 'You see, Job,' says Elihu, 'your problem is that you are viewing God as if he were simply a man writ large, as if he were nothing but a capricious spiteful tyrant acting without reason. Just because *we* cannot immediately see what that reason is doesn't mean that there isn't one. God's time-scale and concerns are much bigger than ours and we need to remember that.'

THE POINT OF PAIN

Secondly, following through this line of thought, Elihu suggests an altogether different perspective for understanding suffering. Instead of looking back for some sort of cause for suffering and asking, 'Is this suffering due to Job's sin or God's injustice (when in fact it is neither)?', Elihu suggests that it might be more helpful to look forward and identify a purpose. In other words if God is good and almighty, what we need to ask is what possible good could there be in him allowing us to suffer like this? And the answer Elihu gives is that it is part of God's way of correcting us, and preventing us from going off the rails and ending in hell, 'to turn man from wrongdoing and keep him from pride, to preserve his soul from the pit' (33:17-18). In verse 19 he speaks of a man being 'chastened on a bed of pain'. Later he says that God makes people 'listen to correction' and 'speaks to them in their affliction' (36:10, 15). Job has already complained that God has not spoken, but Elihu suggests he is speaking 'now one way, now another (33:14) and is speaking to Job through suffering. Job's other friends insisted that God should primarily be thought of as a judge, whereas Elihu suggests that he should be thought of as a teacher: 'Who is a teacher like him?' (36:22). In other words, it is too narrow a view to think of all suffering as retribution, may it not be that some suffering is God's instruction?

A few years ago there was a television documentary series called 'Commando', a programme about the training which goes into making a Royal Marine. It was simply terrifying! A casual observer who knew nothing about what the instructors were trying to achieve might have come to the conclusion that they simply hated the recruits. The observer would have seen the instructors physically hitting and yelling at these young men as they did a twenty-mile cross-country run with seventy pounds on their backs. Even if one of the recruits sprains an ankle or breaks a bone, it is nothing which a few pain-killers cannot put right! It all looks very sadistic. But then the instructors explain what they were hoping to achieve, that the reason why they put these men through such a grilling regime is to produce the best soldiers possible, knowing that their lives and the lives of others may well depend upon the training they have received. It was not retribution they were involved in, but instruction.

The Bible teaches that such is God's purpose for his people, people like Job, people he loves. In fact, the more favoured we are, the more he will use suffering to knock off our rough edges and discipline us, indeed humble us in order to make us into the sort of person he will have us be. We are all prone to pride, thinking we can manage our lives by ourselves, even as Christians. Sometimes we are so stubborn or slow that we do not seriously heed what God would say to us through the Scriptures and so God will speak to us through the 'megaphone of pain', as C. S. Lewis put it, to get our attention. Through suffering we are rightly reminded that we are dependent upon him for our very breath; that life and health are not rights but gifts, but also we are reminded that we should not be so preoccupied with the gifts that we forget the Giver. Sometimes we need our faulty thinking about God to be corrected, as did Job. For all his piety, events did expose this one weakness in his thinking, that he was willing to entertain the idea that God was unjust, and if nothing else his suffering revealed this so that it could be put right. The writer to the Hebrews says:

Endure hardship as discipline; God is treating you as sons. For what son is not disciplined by his father? ... God disciplines us for our good, that we may share in his holiness. No discipline seems pleasant at the time, but painful. Later on, however, it produces a harvest of righteousness and peace for those who have been trained by it (12:7-11).

We have to admit that this is an idea which is alien to modern ears, including Christian ones. We live in a culture where pleasure is prized above all else and where pain is to be avoided at all costs. We expect that everything should come to us with the greatest of ease and the minimum of discomfort. The result is that we expect the Christian life to be easy. The idea that something, such as having a personal relationship with God, might be so valuable that it is worth undergoing some trouble to get it, grates with many in the church, young and old. Why bother coming to church every Sunday, why bother with the hard graft of Bible study or listening to a sermon, why put up with the discipline of prayer or finding ways of serving God in his church which cost in terms of time and effort? We may not always voice it that way but, as we look around many of our churches today, that is the message coming across loud and clear. In this sort of cultural climate we can expect God all the more to shake us out of our complacency and pride by putting us through the mill. We may put it like this: God doesn't want spoilt little brats who think that he owes them a favour, rather he wants loving obedient children who will trust him come what may. Now the question is, which are we going to be?

We can be like sulky children, locking ourselves away in our room, building up resentment towards God for the way he is treating us, refusing to open the door in response to his knocking. Elihu warns Job that he is in danger of letting this happen to him: 'Beware of turning to evil, which you seem to prefer to affliction' (36:21). Or we can be like obedient children who, while expressing the hurt and the pain, nevertheless in the midst of difficulty will ask, 'Lord, what are you teaching me through this?'

GOD IN THE DOCK?

But even that is not enough for Job. He wants to hear from God. And that is precisely what happens, but not in the way Job hoped for: 'Who is this that darkens my counsel with words without knowledge? Brace yourself like a man; I will question you, and you shall answer me' (38:2). Like many people today Job was expecting God to answer a few questions about the appalling way he was running his world. It was God who was to be put into the dock as far as Job was concerned. But the situation is rightly reversed. It is Job who is put in the dock and he is required to answer a few questions to God, questions which would make even the most adept Mastermind contestant shrivel in the big black chair: 'Where were you when I laid the earth's foundation? Tell me, if you understand. Have you ever given orders to the morning, or shown the dawn its place? Have you entered the storehouses of the snow or seen the storehouses of the hail, which I reserve for times of trouble? Can you bind the beautiful Pleiades? Can you loose the cords of Orion? Can you bring forth the constellations in their seasons ...?' Job is barraged with question after question. 'What about the animals? Do you provide for them, Job? Have you got so great a mind that out of nothing you could come up with such a strange looking bird as an ostrich? You think you are so wise, Job, and I am so useless!' Job had wanted an interview with the Almighty, and that is precisely what he got.

But God's defence wasn't quite as Job expected. At the first pause Job answers: 'I am unworthy – how can I reply to you. I put my hand over my mouth' (40:4). In those days the primary aim of someone involved in a lawsuit was not to convince the judge or jury of his innocence, but his accuser, so that he would withdraw his case and acknowledge defeat by placing his hand over his mouth. That is what happened to Job, his case against God collapsed like a stack of cards.

But God hasn't finished yet. 'Brace yourself like a man; I will question you, and you shall answer *me*' (40:7). Then comes the blistering questions which lie at the heart of Job's big mistake and his rebellion and, I would suggest, ours:

'Would you discredit my justice?
   Would you condemn me to justify yourself?

Do you have an arm like God's,
    and can your voice thunder like his?
Then adorn yourself with glory and splendour,
    and clothe yourself in honour and majesty'
                (40:8-9).

In other words, 'Just who do you think you are, Job – God? To protest your innocence is one thing, but to act so high and mighty that you accuse me of injustice is another. In order to make the right judgement upon God and what he is doing you have to have a lot more wisdom, a lot more knowledge than you do have. You have not been able to answer one of my questions, Job, questions to which I know all the answers. Does it not therefore occur to you that I might, just might, have the answer to why I have permitted you to suffer? If you cannot comprehend the intricacies of the creation which you can see, then can you honestly expect to grasp all the mysteries of suffering which are hidden? Of course not, only I, God, can do that.'

What is more, why should we assume that God owes us an explanation as to why he allows suffering, any more than he owes us an explanation as to why he made the ostrich. While it may be true that we can't see why he should design so peculiar a bird, no doubt God had plenty of good reasons for doing so, if only known to himself. Could not the same be said for suffering? More to the point, is it not reasonable to *trust* a God who has both the wisdom and the power to create so mind-boggling a universe, even if we may not be able to understand all the whys and wherefores of what happens in it?

Job finally realised what he had done wrong. His mistake, and ours, is to think that we are privy to *all* the facts, when we are not, and so draw the wrong conclusions from an inadequate data base – that God is not good, that God does not care, that God does not speak. And our response should be that of Job's, not to rise up in arrogance and demand that God explain everything to us, but to repent of our presumption that we know better than God, and fall down in worship.

> 'I know that you can do all things;
>> no plan of yours can be thwarted.
> You asked, "Who is this that obscures my counsel without knowledge?"
>> Surely I spoke of things I did not understand,
>> things too wonderful for me to know....
> Therefore I despise myself
>> and repent in dust and ashes' (42:2-3, 6).

I have a friend who teaches at a University at which I was chaplain. When he and his wife first arrived they were not Christians. He would often come around and argue why he couldn't believe – each time we went through all the evidence. One night I went around to see them and put it to them that the time for arguing was over, they knew that Christianity was true and they knew what they had to do. The sense of the presence of God in that room was quite unmistakable. About one o'clock in the morning, after I had left, they both committed their lives to Christ.

Soon after, his wife became pregnant. In June, Adam was born. A week later he was dead – he had a congenital heart defect. Remember this couple had been Christians only a few months when this happened. I took the funeral, which was simply heartbreaking as the little white coffin was brought in. My friends could have insisted that they had a right to know why, and, having received no answer, might have thrown in the faith. But they didn't. They knew that such an answer was not available to them. He, being a biologist, certainly knew of the grandeur of God's creation, and as he held his baby son in his arms for the last time, he knew about the miracle of birth. But as they reflected on what it was like to lose a son, it was the knowledge that God also knew what it was like to lose a Son that made the difference. From the standpoint of those around the cross, Calvary did not make sense, but God's plans were far greater than anyone could have imagined, as events later proved.

Did this young Christian couple know that God loved them and loved their baby? Yes, they did. Did they know that God had reasons for putting them through so much grief? Yes, they did. And why? Because in Jesus they had *more than sufficient reason to trust the God who knew why.*

Chapter 5

ALL'S WELL THAT ENDS WELL

Job 42

Here is part of a parable told by Professor Basil Mitchell:
In time of war in an occupied country, a member of
the resistance one night meets a stranger who deeply
impresses him. They spend that night together in
conversation. The stranger tells the partisan that he
himself is on the side of the resistance – indeed that
he is in command of it, and urges the partisan to have
faith in him no matter what happens. The partisan
is utterly convinced at that meeting of the stranger's
sincerity and constancy and undertakes to trust him.

They never meet in conditions of intimacy again.
But sometimes the stranger is seen helping members of the resistance, and the partisan is grateful
and says to his friends, 'He is on our side.' Sometimes he is seen in the uniform of the police hand-
ing over patriots to the occupying power. On these
occasions his friends murmur against him: but the
partisan still says, 'He is on our side.' He still believes that, in spite of appearances, the stranger did
not deceive him. Sometimes he asks the stranger
for help and receives it. He is thankful. Sometimes

he asks and does not receive it. Then he says, 'The stranger knows best.'[1]

As we come to the end of our study of Job, the meaning of that parable is obvious. For in essence that is the lesson that Job had to learn, and, according to the New Testament, it is the lesson we too are to learn, namely, that in spite of appearances to the contrary, 'The Stranger' – God – knows best and we are called to trust him.

THE CALL TO TRUST

Job's own attitude began with a mixture of self-pity and self-assertion. As his life was devastated by one calamity after another, not surprisingly Job sank into himself in grief. Then, in spite of his wife's advice to curse God and die, he insisted on defending his own innocence. By contrast the attitude recommended by Job's three friends was self-accusation. 'Come on, Job,' they said, 'admit that you are suffering because of your sin. This is God's judgement upon you, repent and it will soon turn out alright.' But Job refused to be bullied into signing such a false confession and denying his integrity – he was innocent. Then the fourth friend, Elihu, appears on the scene and he urges upon Job yet another attitude to adopt, that of self-discipline. He pleads with Job to see that there is some purpose in his pain, not retribution but instruction, to recognise that in some measure this

---

1. Basil Mitchell, 'Theology and Falsification' in *New Essays in Philosophical Theology*, A. Flew and A. MacIntyre (eds.), (SCM, 1958).

is God's way of discipling and correcting us. Then finally it is God who speaks and the only attitude which is left open to Job is self-surrender, falling before God in reverence, awe and humility. And that, of course, is the attitude which God commends.

Many people feel that the story should have ended in 42:6 with Job falling on his knees and saying, 'Therefore I despise myself and repent in dust and ashes.' It seems almost incredible to some that, after such a robust wrestling with the problem of suffering in which the most forthright candour has been expressed in challenging traditionally cherished beliefs, the writer should throw it all away by rounding the story off with a fairy tale ending of the 'they all lived happily ever after' variety. Fairy stories may have happy endings, but real life very often does not. To tell us that Job ends up with *more* than he had originally undermines the main argument of the book, because it gives the impression that the retributive theory is correct after all: be naughty and you get punished, be good and you get rewarded; as if God were trying to buy off Job, placating him with a few goodies, saying, 'I am not so nasty after all, I am really kind, you know.'

On a superficial reading of the text some may well think that. But I would suggest that no other ending would have been possible. For if we had simply finished with God's encounter with Job, God's wisdom and power may have been vindicated, but not his justice, which after all was Job's main concern.

In this epilogue we see both the justice of God and the grace of God meeting each other perfectly.

MORE THAN JUSTICE

To begin with we see God's justice in the way he deals with Job's three friends.

> After the LORD had said these things to Job, he said to Eliphaz the Temanite, 'I am angry with you and your two friends, because you have not spoken of me what is right, as my servant Job has. So now take seven bulls and seven rams and go to my servant Job and sacrifice a burnt offering for yourselves. My servant Job will pray for you, and I will accept his prayer and not deal with you according to your folly. You have not spoken of me what is right, as my servant Job has.' So Eliphaz the Temanite, Bildad the Shuhite and Zophar the Naamathite did what the LORD told them; and the LORD accepted Job's prayer.
> (42:7-9).

Do you remember how Job had to put up with so much slander, how he was vilified over and over again and his character brought into question? Do you recall how he was accused of being a hypocrite, of harbouring wicked thoughts, of gaining his wealth through sharp practice? That had been so painful. But the more he protested, the more convinced his accusers became that he was hiding something. He desperately needed someone to come to his defence; someone who knew the truth and would testify to his innocence. But there was only one who could do that, and that was God.

And that is precisely what we see God doing here. He rounds on Job's three counsellors in anger because of what they have said. They may have been sincere in their beliefs, but sincerity is no defence, they were plain wrong. They were wrong in what they had said about Job and, more to the point, by implication they were wrong in what they had said about God. It is ironic that these three thought they were representing God, when in fact all the time they were misrepresenting him. At the end of the day their theology reduces God to an inconsistent tyrant. They claim he works out everything in terms of just retribution, but it is obvious that the theory does not fit with the facts, so the result is that God appears to be an arbitrary monster, punishing some but not others. And that view of God is simply not right. We need to be very careful that we do not find ourselves misrepresenting God, perhaps by focusing on his justice to the exclusion of his love or, as is more likely today, focusing on his love to the exclusion of his justice. Such an appalling false image will not go unnoticed.

Job was vindicated in time, but that is not always the way it works out for Christians. We may well be misunderstood and misrepresented, even by some of our so-called Christian friends and we will have to live with that pain. But there will come a day when everything will be out in the open, when there will be a clearing of the books – and that will be judgement day. Then the record will be put straight. Those lies and half truths, those sneers that we may have had to endure, not only because we have owned the name of Jesus Christ but because we had the guts to put our faith into practice when other Christians faded away, will be put right. It is not for us to be preoccupied with trying to clear our name and justify ourselves. Instead we are to get on with what God has called us to do and leave the judging up to him. He will see to it that if we are in the right it will be made known, so let's not worry about it unduly.

Here are the wise words of the apostle Paul on this point (a man who like Job knew what it was to be misrepresented and slandered by his friends): 'Therefore judge nothing before the appointed time; wait till the Lord comes. He will bring to light what is hidden in darkness and will expose the motives of men's hearts. At that time each will receive his praise from God' (1 Cor. 4:5).

AMAZING GRACE

Not only do we see God's justice at work but also his grace – God's *undeserved* mercy. Far from God exacting his pound of flesh (as Job's friends deserved) God, by his very action of providing a way for their sin to be dealt with, reveals his kindness. If God had treated them according to strict justice, as they had been arguing God must treat everyone, then they would have been wiped out. But he didn't. Sin had to be covered over, and that involves a sacrifice. What is more, someone is needed to intercede for sinners, someone of good standing, someone whom God will hear, and the only one who filled all the requirements was the one they had been slandering as a liar and a cheat – Job.

To Job's credit, he did pray for them and God accepted his prayer. For Job there was no malice, no resentment against these men who, with their searing accusations, had heaped upon him more agonies than he could bear. Instead, there was nothing but kindness. I wonder how many of us would have had the grace to behave in that way? Job is most impressive, isn't he? Often, when someone says a bad word against us we don't forget it, and we make sure they don't forget it either. But not Job, he prays for them. And immediately we are reminded of another sufferer who prayed for those who laughed at him and taunted him and spat at him in his greatest hour of need. Jesus prayed, 'Father, forgive them for they don't know what they are doing.' Indeed, is there not in Job's response at the very least a distant echo of the way God was to demonstrate beyond any reasonable doubt that he is both just and merciful by providing the supreme sacrifice for *our* sins, in the body of his own Son at Calvary (Rom. 3:26)? God is not inconsistent, as Job's comforters' logic implied, God does not ignore sin, he deals with it by absorbing it to himself in his dear Son, so that we might go free.

What is more, we also see God's grace shown to Job in the way his former life is not simply restored but surpassed: 'After Job had prayed for his friends, the LORD made him prosperous again and gave him twice as much as he had before' (42:10).

It is important that we don't see this as compensation for all that Job has suffered. Remember how right at the beginning it was Satan's taunt that the only reason why Job was so religious was because of what he could get out of it, that there was some ulterior motive, that he was in it for what he could get? By taking everything away from Job, God demonstrated that the taunt was a lie. Even when he had nothing to entice him to believe in God, Job still trusted him. It wasn't a matter of Job thinking, 'Well, if I just hang on to the end there might be some goodies in store.' Job didn't know what the outcome was going to be, in fact it was more than likely he thought he was going to die. But nevertheless he still trusted God – the Stranger knows best.

Is not this a pointer to heaven? This book of Job appeared early on in the history of Israel, before any clear ideas about heaven and the after-life had been revealed. Just as it was only by God vindicating Job in time rather than at the end of time that justice was seen to be done, so it is only by God blessing Job in this world as well as in the next that it can be shown that the righteous life is worth it after all.

Although we are not to follow God simply because of what we can get out of it, nevertheless it does make very good sense to follow God because it is the most rewarding life. It is rewarding in this life because we have a personal relationship with God and have a direction in life – 'life in its fullness' as Jesus said. Even though materially we might not have much to show for it, spiritually you cannot beat it.

But it is also rewarding in the next life because we shall then experience the complete joy of being a Christian rather than the eternal torment of not being one. Here we see Job, in his own way, finding out that truth for himself. God does honour those who honour him. He does not come to us empty handed for having suffered for him and remaining faithful to him when the going was tough. It is right for a believer who is going through the flames of suffering to have his sight on the consolation of heaven. Listen to these words from the writer to the Hebrews, writing to young believers who were being put through the mill because they stood out as Christians:

> Let us fix our eyes on Jesus, the author and perfecter of our faith, *who for the joy set before him* endured the cross, scorning its shame, and sat down at the right hand of the throne of God (12:2).

Even Jesus was given the courage and the strength to endure the most appalling suffering and cruelty by setting his heart on the joys that were to come. The joy not only of returning to his heavenly Father and to that wonderful relationship of love and glory he had cherished from all eternity; the joy not simply of ruling with his Father over the universe they had created; but the surpassing joy of seeing many spiritual children come to glory through faith in him. Job had his offspring out of adversity; well, Jesus has his – Christian believers. Isn't it moving to know that he thought we were worth it? As the eternal Son of God looked down the long corridors of time from heaven and saw each one of his chosen children's faces, he said, 'For them I will go to the cross, for them I will treat with contempt all the hurt and ridicule that people will throw at me, why I will even bear their guilt if it is the only way they can be set free. Yes, for that joy of seeing them in heaven, I *willingly* suffer.'

FAITH IN A SUFFERING GOD

But it may be that you still remain unconvinced. Like the writer Philip Yancey, you say, 'If God is truly in charge, somehow connected to all the world's suffering, why is he so capricious, unfair? Is he the cosmic sadist who delights in watching us squirm?'[2] Well, is he? We may say, 'It's alright for God, secure in the comfort of heaven, but what does he know about suffering, what does he know about soul-destroying devastation?'

But surely the Christian must reply that God knows far more than any of us. In many ways Job

---

2. Philip Yancey, *Where is God When it Hurts?* (Zondervan, 1977).

is a type, a pointer to one who was yet to come. Someone else who was also known as God's servant, someone else whom Satan wanted to test. But whereas with Job, God did not allow Satan to test him to the point of death, with this other servant Satan was allowed to go all the way. No suffering was considered to be too great to be inflicted upon this innocent man. If Job was reduced to living on the local ash heap, Jesus was stripped naked, and nailed up like a scarecrow on the local rubbish heap.

You find it difficult to believe in God because of suffering, I find I *have* to believe in God because of suffering – the suffering of Jesus. It is in him that we see a God who really does care, who cares enough to spare us from the eternal suffering our sins demand, that he suffers them in our place. Do you really want to begin to plumb the mystery of suffering? Then you need to look to that lonely, twisted, tortured figure on the cross, nails through hands and feet, back lacerated, limbs wrenched, brow bleeding from thorn pricks, mouth dry and intolerably thirsty, plunged in God-forsaken darkness. That is where you look. And if you want to see how such unbelievable suffering can be transformed into infinite good, then look on to an empty tomb and to a garden in which stands the crucified Conqueror, with the palms of his hands outstretched, offering the gift of eternal life, and saying to you, 'Believe and trust in me.'

Chapter 6

A Very Peculiar Form of Suffering

Psalm 42

[1] As the deer pants for streams of water,
    so my soul pants for you, O God.
[2] My soul thirsts for God, for the living God.
    When can I go and meet with God?
[3] My tears have been my food
    day and night,
while men say to me all day long,
    "Where is your God?"

[4] These things I remember
    as I pour out my soul:
how I used to go with the multitude,
    leading the procession to the house of God,
with shouts of joy and thanksgiving
    among the festive throng.

[5] Why are you downcast, O my soul?
    Why so disturbed within me?
Put your hope in God,
    for I will yet praise him,
    my Saviour and [6] my God.

My soul is downcast within me;
    therefore I will remember you
from the land of Jordan,
    the heights of Hermon – from Mount Mizar.

[7] Deep calls to deep
    in the roar of your waterfalls;

all your waves and breakers
   have swept over me.

[8] By day the Lord directs his love,
   at night his song is with me –
   a prayer to the God of my life.

[9] I say to God my Rock,
   "Why have you forgotten me?
Why must I go about mourning,
   oppressed by the enemy?"
[10] My bones suffer mortal agony
   as my foes taunt me,
saying to me all day long,
   "Where is your God?"

[11] Why are you downcast, O my soul?
   Why so disturbed within me?
Put your hope in God,
   for I will yet praise him,
   my Saviour and my God.

'If I were a better Christian I wouldn't get so depressed' is a statement I have heard many times from believers when they feel discouraged or experience a profound set-back. I guess that this is not so surprising, given the way some Christian books and certain speakers foster the impression that if you are depressed it is symptomatic of lack of faith, whereas the normal Christian life is one of unrelenting victory. Instead, we are urged to 'name and claim God's promises'. 'God is the only tranquillizer I need,' said one viewer who phoned in to a TV chat show on which appeared a well-known Christian psychiatrist. The result is that those of us who are prone to melancholy from time to time are made to feel a little inferior, being placed amongst the 'spiritually challenged'.

It therefore comes as a relief to discover that many of the Bible writers knew only too well what it was like to suffer depression. One immediately thinks of Job undergoing the torment of bereavement and illness, or Jeremiah whose lack of response amongst his hearers to God's Word made him wish he had never been born. Even the greatest amongst them, in the agony of fear in the garden of Gethsemane, was practically rendered immobile by the great weight of depression which impressed upon him. Amongst God's people, depression is far from a rarity. Martin Luther[1], David Brainerd[2], C. H. Spurgeon[3], Amy Carmichael[4] and David Watson[5] and many others all had to wrestle with what Winston Churchill called the 'black dog' – depression.

In this chapter we consider the state of a man who is undergoing what can only be described as spiritual depression – the writer of Psalm 42. As we listen in to his mental wrestlings we not only discover much with which we can identify but also learn some valuable lessons as to how we might cope with this sort of depression. In fact, we discover that

1. Dolina MacCuish, *Luther and His Katie* (CFP, 1974).
2. See *The Works of Jonathan Edwards*, Volume 2, pp. 313-447 for an account of Brainerd's life (Banner of Truth, 1988).
3. See E. Skoglund, *Coping*, pp. 12-38 (Regal Books, 1980).
4. ibid.
5. David Watson, *You Are My God* (Hodder & Stoughton, 1983).

there are three vital stages through which we must travel in order to cope with spiritual depression: own up, think through, and pull together.

OWN UP

First of all, we are to admit how we feel. Isn't it striking how transparently honest this man is about his emotions, he simply lets his feelings flow out before God. There is no British stiff upper lip, no slipping on the plastic Christian mask, just the open admission of feeling utterly dreadful and down.

Just take a look at the sort of imagery he uses to describe his mental and spiritual state. He is *parched*:

> As the deer pants for streams of water,
>   so my soul pants for you, O God.
> My soul thirsts for God, for the living God.
>   When can I go and meet with God?

Think back to those pictures of the Gulf War and the troops languishing in the hot Arabian desert where there is nothing as far as the eye can see but blistering sand and clear blue skies. Imagine being placed there with no water, and dehydration setting in. You are weak, all you can think about is relief which can come through one glass of ice-cool liquid. That is how this man felt spiritually. He longed for God as a thirsting man would long for water. Being a Jew that meant meeting with God in his temple: 'These things I remember as I pour out my soul: how I used to go with the multitude, leading the procession to the house of God' (v. 4). Of course, the Psalmist believes that God is accessible everywhere, otherwise he wouldn't be praying at all, but he believes that God dwells amongst his people in a special way when they are gathered together in the temple or, as we would put it, meeting as a church. Now he is cut off from all of that and it is driving him quite literally to despair.

What is more, he is off his food, as so very often happens when we feel like this: 'My tears have been my food day and night' (v. 3). He can't eat, he is restless, unable to sleep and he can't stop crying. It may come in waves, one minute he feels in control and the next moment for no obvious reason he finds himself sobbing uncontrollably, he just can't help it and he is not ashamed to admit this to God.

But what makes matters worse, if they could be worse, are the taunts and jibes he has to endure from onlookers who take delight in pointing out the utter futility of his believing in God: 'My tears have been my food day and night, while men say to me all day long, "Where is your God?" ' (v. 3). If only he could point to something, some sign of God at work and say, 'But look, he isn't like that, he does care', then that would be some consolation. But he feels he can't. His opponents seem to have both reason and experience on their side. 'So much for your faith,' they say. 'What is the point in having a God who is not there when you need him?' How does one respond? It hurts, salt is rubbed into an already festering wound.

But not only does this man feel as if he is in a spiritual wasteland, he also feels as if he is drowning emotionally: 'Deep calls to deep in the roar of your waterfalls; all your waves and breakers have swept over me' (v. 7). This is not a contradiction with what he says earlier about being in a drought-like situation, it is something which ties in with experience. Whereas thirsting indicates the absence of something – lack of peace of mind or the absence of God – drowning indicates the helplessness we feel when we are 'out of our depths'. The whole experience of depression is so overwhelming that we feel we can't keep our heads above water, we are simply going under.

There is a very important principle here which we need to grasp if we are to cope with these sorts of feelings, and that is the need to admit them. Instead of shrugging them off and saying, 'They don't matter' or, worse still, denying them altogether, we have to face them and express them. One thing that psychologists observe is that very often depression is associated with repressed anger. One psychotherapist even called depression a state of 'frozen rage'. If those angry feelings get bottled up in a Christian, then it is all too easy for them to get transferred to God. Inwardly we feel furious with him, indignant, indeed, exasperated. And if that is so, then like the Psalmist we do need to tell God and share how we feel about him: 'I say to God my Rock, "Why have you forgotten me? Why must I go about mourning, oppressed by the enemy?" My bones suffer mortal agony as my foes taunt me, saying to me all day long, "Where is your God?"' (vv. 9-10).

William Blake wrote a little poem which puts it quite well:

> I was angry with my friend.
> I told my wrath,
> My wrath did end.
> I was angry with my foe.
> I told it not,
> My wrath did grow.

That is true. If we feel angry towards God and tell him, then the anger can be dealt with. But if we don't, it will simply grow. Therefore, it is vital we tell what we feel rather than repress it. Depression is often anger turned inward. Far better to turn it outwards and express those concerns to God.

THINK THROUGH

Simply venting our feelings, however, is not enough, we must also engage the mind – think through. That is precisely what this man does in verse 5: 'Why are you downcast, O my soul? Why so disturbed within me? Put your hope in God, for I will yet praise him, my Saviour and my God.'

In his classic book, *Spiritual Depression*, the former Harley Street physician-turned-preacher, Dr Martyn Lloyd-Jones, writes:

> We must talk to ourselves instead of letting ourselves talk to us. The main trouble in this whole matter of spiritual depression is that we

allow our self to talk to us instead of talking to the self. You have to take yourself in hand, you have to address yourself, question yourself and say 'Hope thou in God,' instead of muttering away in this depressed and unhappy way.[6]

How does he talk to himself, and move himself on to put his hope in God?

First of all, he begins by *remembering*, looking back to former times of corporate worship: 'These things I remember as I pour out my soul: how I used to go with the multitude, leading the procession to the house of God, with shouts of joy and thanksgiving among the festive throng' (verse 4). Admittedly, this would have been a bitter-sweet experience. Those were the good times, times of meeting with God and his people, the great occasions when he would have heard the Word of God read with all its promises, when he would have lifted his heart with other believers in prayer and praise. So he thinks about them, ponders them.

It is significant that he begins with corporate worship rather than private personal experience, because it introduces a certain objectivity into the situation. If he focused solely on his private religious life, he could open himself to the doubt that it was all make-believe. But by thinking about other people, and God's Word being proclaimed

---

6. D. M. Lloyd-Jones, *Spiritual Depression, its causes and cures* (Pickering and Inglis, 1974).

– that is more difficult to dismiss, after all, not all of those people who were with him on those occasions could be deluded. In other words, the Christian faith and the reality of God remain true regardless of how we feel. It is not the case that God is as 'real as I feel', that is too subjective. Unfortunately much Christian despair today is caused because people do measure the truth and reality of God in these terms, which is hopeless. Now can you see why regularly meeting with others, coming along to church, getting involved in Bible study groups are vitally important? Because they provide the objectivity and strength we all need to keep on trusting in God, to give that open perspective that Christianity is true. Then we can look back to them, and remember them when we find ourselves alone and in trouble.

This principle is also brought out in verse 8: 'I call you to mind day and night how the LORD used to show me his covenant love: I would sing his praise and pray to God who was my life' (my translation). He speaks of God's covenant love, that is, the promise of his grace as he has declared it through his Word, or, as we would put it today, that promise of his love as we have it in the gospel. God has spoken, God has promised that he will love us with an everlasting love, that in spite of our sin he will never let us go. That is a fact, a truth God has declared, and he does not lie or renege on his promises.

A passage which sheds light on this is Romans 8:37. There Paul has listed all the difficulties a Christian can face in this life – such as persecution, suffering, starvation – circumstances which would normally cause us to question God's love. Having reviewed all of these things Paul then writes: 'No, in all these things we are more than conquerors through him [Jesus] who loved us.' We would not write it like that today, we would write: 'No, in all these things we are more than conquerors through him who *loves* us.' But Paul uses a tense that denotes a 'once or all event'. And the reason is not difficult to grasp. For where do we see God's love displayed so clearly and exhaustively but on the cross. It is to this historic event that we are to look for the assurance that God loved us and will continue to love us, a love which began in eternity, which took the Son of God to the cross to atone for our sins in history, and which will take us into heaven. In our mind's eye we continually need to go back there and say, 'If God has done all this for me, and he has, will he abandon me now?' And the answer is, 'No, of course not.' God will do no such thing.

But that assurance does not come automatically, we need to think about it, to reason it through, to soak our minds in Bible truth and live our lives in the light of its glories. As Dr Lloyd-Jones put it, 'Talk to your self instead of letting your self talk to you.' Feelings come and go, personal experiences are so flighty, but truth cannot be so easily eroded.

That is why God has given us a Bible; from it we can get the reassurance of the faithfulness of God; therefore ponder it, imbibe it and rejoice in it.

PULL TOGETHER

Finally we come to the third stage, pull together. It is vital that we recognise that this comes right at the end. We should never say to anyone who is going through this sort of crisis, 'Snap out of it, pull yourself together.' That is both cruel and pastorally insensitive. We must be with them, support them, and help them express how they feel, together with the gentle encouragement of Scripture. Only then with God's help is there a resolve to move on.

In verse 11, is the Psalmist saying that at some point in the future he will praise God, or is he saying that he will start to praise God immediately?

> Why are you downcast, O my soul?
>> Why so disturbed within me?
> Put your hope in God,
>> for I will yet praise him,
>> my Saviour and my God.

He has seen why he is downcast, what circumstances have made him feel cut off from God's people and the means of grace, his being taunted by his enemies. But then he lifts his eyes beyond the immediate, and gains the larger perspective of a God who is a rock, who is full of covenant love, who has shown his faithfulness in the past, and so he resolves, 'I will put my hope in him, his is *my* Saviour and my God.'

This is an act of the will, based upon truth and if the feelings follow, all well and good; if not, then we still must go on.

I mentioned earlier the depression suffered by the great Reformer Martin Luther. At one period in his life he went through a particularly severe depression. He was being persecuted by the church, his son was severely ill, his wife was going through a difficult pregnancy, and the devil was tempting him in an appalling manner; so understandably he began to doubt whether God really did care. This is how one biographer describes his response:

> No matter how long or severe his depressions might be, and they were to recur throughout his life, he still managed to get through an amazing amount of work. He felt that in some way they were inevitable if one were to have a real understanding of things spiritual, for 'he does not know what hope is who has never been subject to temptations'. At the same time they were to be avoided if at all possible. But how? As the spiritual pioneer of his age he could never look to others for affirmation nor could he ever find anything in himself on which to ground his hope. His affirmation must come from God but he could not know him directly, so in the final analysis he must be rooted in the Scriptures. That is why he gave such a priority to the translation of the Bible; it was so that each could find truth for himself. At other times he in his down-to-earth way said the best way to combat despondency was to go out among the people, laugh, joke and sing, get involved, even get angry; do something useful

such as harness a horse and spread manure on the fields. Music was especially effective for the Devil is a morose being who flees music.[7]

Wise advice from a wise man on a very peculiar form of suffering.

---

7. As above, *Luther and His Katie*.

Chapter 7

It's Not Fair

Psalm 73

[1] Surely God is good to Israel,
　　to those who are pure in heart.

[2] But as for me, my feet had almost slipped;
　　I had nearly lost my foothold.
[3] For I envied the arrogant
　　when I saw the prosperity of the wicked.

[4] They have no struggles;
　　their bodies are healthy and strong.
[5] They are free from the burdens common to man;
　　they are not plagued by human ills.
[6] Therefore pride is their necklace;
　　they clothe themselves with violence.
[7] From their callous hearts comes iniquity;
　　the evil conceits of their minds know no limits.

[8] They scoff, and speak with malice;
　　in their arrogance they threaten oppression.
[9] Their mouths lay claim to heaven,
　　and their tongues take possession of the earth.
[10] Therefore their people turn to them
　　and drink up waters in abundance.
[11] They say, "How can God know?
　　Does the Most High have knowledge?"
[12] This is what the wicked are like -
　　always carefree, they increase in wealth.

[13] Surely in vain have I kept my heart pure;
　　in vain have I washed my hands in innocence.

[14] All day long I have been plagued;
  I have been punished every morning.
[15] If I had said, "I will speak thus,"
  I would have betrayed your children.
[16] When I tried to understand all this,
  it was oppressive to me
[17] till I entered the sanctuary of God;
  then I understood their final destiny.

[18] Surely you place them on slippery ground;
  you cast them down to ruin.
[19] How suddenly are they destroyed,
  completely swept away by terrors!
[20] As a dream when one awakes,
  so when you arise, O Lord,
  you will despise them as fantasies.

[21] When my heart was grieved
  and my spirit embittered,
[22] I was senseless and ignorant;
  I was a brute beast before you.

[23] Yet I am always with you;
  you hold me by my right hand.
[24] You guide me with your counsel,
  and afterward you will take me into glory.
[25] Whom have I in heaven but you?
  And earth has nothing I desire besides you.
[26] My flesh and my heart may fail,
  but God is the strength of my heart
  and my portion forever.
[27] Those who are far from you will perish;
  you destroy all who are unfaithful to you.
[28] But as for me, it is good to be near God.
  I have made the Sovereign LORD my refuge;
  I will tell of all your deeds.

The cry, 'It's not fair', is a plea which is not restricted to the children's playground when one of the little darlings decides to bend the rules of the game to suit himself. In fact, it is a heartfelt cry heard in every area of life. 'It's not fair that I should work so hard for that promotion only to be passed over for someone less able but whose face just happens to fit.' 'It's not fair that the loan shark whose financial trickery has wrecked the lives of countless families is a picture of health while that former nurse who has spent all her life caring for people is struck down with Alzheimers.' And so on.

If you feel like that then you are in the company of our Psalmist who would be quick to agree with you. 'Too true, life isn't fair,' he says, 'the wicked seem to prosper at the expense of the honest hard worker, while those who try to keep their noses clean simply get the rough end of the stick.' But what makes this psalm all the more poignant is that it is written by a man who believes in a just and good God and, initially at least, that belief makes what he sees worse, not better, because he finds it difficult to come to terms with how a good God can allow the wicked to get away with it. How can he just stand by and let these things happen? If we are honest, we may well have more than a touch of sympathy with that view.

So, let us see how the psalmist handles what is for him, and what may be for us, a crisis of faith.

THE PREMISE

The writer begins with a premise, a basic statement of belief. 'Surely,' he says in verse 1, 'God is good to Israel, to those who are pure in heart.' This is a nonnegotiable item of faith, equivalent to our creed – God is good. What is more, he is especially good to Israel, his chosen people, and to those who are dedicated followers of his, to those who today we would call Christians.

THE PROBLEM

But straightaway he tells us, and indeed tells God in no uncertain terms, that his experience seems to bring that belief into question: 'As for me, my feet had almost slipped; I had nearly lost my foothold [my faith]. For I envied the arrogant' (v. 2). Why was he jealous? Because he 'saw the prosperity of the wicked'. That is the problem. In other words, there is a fundamental contradiction between his faith (what his head believes – that God is good to those who love him) and the facts (what his eyes see – the well-to-do wicked). It doesn't make sense and the result is that his heart is in turmoil. He wants to continue believing in a good God, but what he finds welling up within is envy of the wicked and, worst of all, an increasing resentment towards his Maker.

Look at what he says in verses 4-5:

> They have no struggles;
>   their bodies are healthy and strong.
> They are free from the burdens common to man;
>   they are not plagued by human ills.

Their life is one constant party, claims the Psalmist. They have all the modern labour saving devices, so they are not unduly burdened as the rest of us lesser mortals. Their bodies are a picture of health and no doubt if illness did happen to strike them down, they are paid-up members of BUPA and have access to the best medical care money can buy – money no doubt obtained dishonestly. Why, even when it comes to them having to face the grim reaper, they seem to die peacefully – that is how verse 4 can be translated: 'they have no struggles at death.' Joseph Stalin, the Russian dictator, who alone was responsible for the death over 20 million Russians, died quite peacefully in his bed with a smile on his face. 'Don't tell me life is not fair,' rails the Psalmist, 'Why, even death is not fair!'

What is more, these people's whole life revolves around violence (v. 6). 'They clothe themselves with violence' like a man wrapping himself up in a warm coat to protect himself against the elements. These people protect themselves against hardship by dishing it out: 'They scoff, and speak with malice; in their arrogance they threaten oppression' (v. 8). They feel that they are untouchable, no court can get to them, they are beyond the normal means of justice and however long the arm of the law may be it is not long enough to touch them. It is making our believer quite ill, it is plain demoralising.

It may be that we feel the same as we look out on our society. I have had it said to me over and over again: 'They say crime does not pay, but obviously it does.' Ask the criminals with their diamond rings and gold bracelets whether crime doesn't pay. Ask the person who broke into my former churchwarden's house one Christmas morning whether crime does not pay – he or she was never caught.

But if the influence of such people were somehow constrained, that might make life a little more tolerable. But it isn't, their influence spreads like a cancer, with people actually looking up to them and emulating them, and so getting caught up in this web of evil: 'Therefore their people turn to them and drink up waters in abundance' (v. 10). And, to add insult to injury, they scoff and tease the believer: 'They say, "How can God know? Does the Most High have knowledge?" ' (v. 11). 'God knows everything, does he? Well, it doesn't seem that way, for why else do they get away with it? So he can't know everything. Or if he does, then he can't be all powerful, otherwise he would have acted by now.'

And so the believer faces the problem that has tormented Christians down the ages, a problem which may be put in the form of our dilemma: If God is good he must wish to abolish evil. If God is all powerful he must be able to abolish evil. But evil exists, therefore he cannot be both good and all powerful. That is the apparent force of the logic: either God is good and wants to get rid of evil but cannot, or he can get rid of evil but does not want to, therefore he cannot be good. That is a painful dilemma for believers. So how does the Psalmist resolve it?

The writer is at least honest. He doesn't bury his head in the sand as some people do and refuse to wrestle with difficult questions like that. No, God respects honesty, *even* honest doubt:

> Surely in vain have I kept my heart pure;
>> in vain have I washed my hands in innocence.
> All day long I have been plagued;
>> I have been punished every morning
>>>> (vv. 13-14).

The man questions his faith. 'What is the point,' he asks, 'of trying to live a good life? It doesn't seem to get you very far, except more and more grief. It has been a total waste of time, pure delusion. God is good to Israel? Come off it. Do unto others as you would have them do unto you? That is a mug's game; no, do others before they do you is more like it.'

Maybe we can identify with such feelings. But we would be wrong if we simply left it there. To express doubts is one thing, to leave them unresolved is another, for if they are not faced and dealt with they will get worse and we could slide into outright unbelief, and that would be tragic.

So having vent his spleen, calmer reflection takes over: 'If I had said, "I will speak thus," I would have betrayed your children' (v. 15). In other words, he is saying, 'Although I may think these things and voice them to you, God, I am not going to be so irresponsible as to voice them to God's people.' Being in a leadership position, as he no doubt was, he was not going to go around upsetting the faith of others. Why, as we read in verse 16, the problem of evil was perplexing enough for him, without it suddenly being dumped onto the delicate shoulders of a young believer: 'When I tried to understand all this, it was oppressive to me.'

When you think about it, that was a very mature thing to do. He at least had the well-being of other believers at heart. He was not going to use the pulpit or the Bible study group to upset their faith by expressing doubts about his own faith. And we too ought to think twice before we give voice to our problems or at least make sure that we have a quiet word with a mature Christian about them. We must be discerning.

There was something else about this man which was impressive: he knew how shamefully he was behaving. We all can behave in a similar manner when things get us down; we simply react, lash out on instinct, being no better than a wild animal: 'When my heart was grieved and my spirit embittered, I was senseless and ignorant; I was a brute beast before you' (vv. 21-22). Instead of allowing God's revelation from his Word to inform our minds and to shape our thoughts, we allow our bitterness to twist our minds. Instead of engaging in evangelical thinking – Bible based thinking – we are taken over by emotional thinking.

A PROPER PERSPECTIVE

What was it that changed his attitude? It was the revelation of God which gave him a proper perspective on things:

When I tried to understand all this,
    it was oppressive to me
till I entered the sanctuary of God;
    then I understood their final destiny.

Surely you place them on slippery ground;
    you cast them down to ruin.
How suddenly are they destroyed,
    completely swept away by terrors!
As a dream when one awakes,
    so when you arise, O Lord,
    you will despise them as fantasies ...

Those who are far from you will perish;
    you destroy all who are unfaithful to you

                    (vv. 16-20, 27).

In other words, it was the perspective of eternity that altered everything, a perspective which had God at the centre. We constantly need to remember that this life is not all there is. Our problems arise when we treat it as if it were. It's a little like watching a film where the villain seems to be getting away literally with murder and we stop the film before it has run to the end and so it seems that there is no justice. But what we have got to do, as it were, is to allow the film to run on until the point where the villain invariably gets his come-uppence.

The awesome fact is that people may escape judgement in the here and now, but they will certainly not escape it in the there and then. People who think that God is not watching, not taking note of evil deeds, had better think again. There is not one hurtful word, not one dishonest act which God does not see and remember. Far from envying such people, we should pity them. Far from wishing we were like them, having what they have, we should be praying that they would become like us. We should be sharing the gospel with them so that they might turn to the Saviour before it is too late. One day God will show his justice in unrelenting fury – Jesus said so – it's called judgement day. But at the moment he is showing his goodness in longsuffering patience, actually giving these people time to repent and change their ways (2 Pet. 3:9).

How then is God good to the pure in heart – the believers?

> Yet I am always with you;
>> you hold me by my right hand.
> You guide me with your counsel,
>> and afterwards you will take me into glory.
> Whom have I in heaven but you?
>> And earth has nothing I desire besides you.
> My flesh and my heart may fail,
>> but God is the strength of my heart
>> and my portion for ever' (23-26).

Which is better? To suffer injustice and hardship in this world with God by your side, or to suffer justice and eternal darkness in the next world with God leaving you on the outside? Oh yes, the corrupt and the violent may have their measure of enjoyment, but what is that compared to the constant, faithful guidance and care of a Father God which he gives to his children – even children who in a fit of depression doubt him and shout at him? Which would you rather have?

One day a woman walked into the office of a well-known Christian counsellor and this is what she said to him: 'Before I came here, I was involved in a life of sexual fun and games and in a real sense felt good. It was exciting. Since I have truly decided to commit myself to Christ, I've found that life has become a struggle. The worldly life was easier and happier than the Christian life. But I wouldn't go back for anything. There is no turning around. I have tasted reality. Painful though it sometimes is, I want more. For the first time in my life I feel truly alive, I'm together. It hurts like blazes, but it's worth it for now I am a whole person.'

It is far better to be a Christian realist having this proper perspective and the love and joy of Christ in your life, than not being a Christian and living an empty fantasy life which one day will be brought to an abrupt end.

If God is good he must wish to abolish evil, if God is all powerful he must be able to abolish evil. We believe he is both good and powerful for, unlike the psalmist, we have the advantage of looking at the problem from this side of the cross. For we can say, looking at that cross, that although as *yet* God may not have abolished evil (although one day he will), he has given evil a decisive blow. What is more, it is at that cross that we see God's goodness and power shown so remarkably, for this is precisely the means he has chosen to forgive us and bring us home to himself. And so we can say with even greater certainty:

> But as for me, it is good to be near God.
> I have made the Sovereign LORD my refuge;
> I will tell of all your deeds (v. 28).

Chapter 8

WHAT DOES JESUS SAY?

Luke 13:1-5

[1]Now there were some present at that time who told Jesus about the Galileans whose blood Pilate had mixed with their sacrifices. [2]Jesus answered, 'Do you think that these Galileans were worse sinners than all the other Galileans because they suffered this way? [3]I tell you, no! But unless you repent, you too will all perish. [4]Or those eighteen who died when the tower in Siloam fell on them – do you think they were more guilty than all the others living in Jerusalem? [5]I tell you, no! But unless you repent, you too will all perish'.

I was eighteen and at home in Wales with my parents and brothers when an urgent plea for help was broadcast on the radio. That very morning a mountain of coal dust, slag and slurry had collapsed and engulfed a primary school in the tiny community of Aberfan. All able-bodied Welshmen were urged to make their way to the village. Clutching spades my father, brothers and I set off too.

The arc lights blazed over the area which had, so recently, echoed to the sounds of children playing, and burly miners wept openly as they worked through the night digging. A hush would descend on the whole site as the cry went out that yet another dead child had been found. Altogether the dead bodies of 116 children and 28 adults were unearthed. The memory of that awful tragedy still lives on in the minds of loved ones and friends.[1]

So writes Lyndon Bowring of the CARE trust.

That tragedy and many more before and since call from any sensitive heart the questions: 'Why? Where was God in all of this? What does God have to say?'

Once Jesus was confronted with similar questions concerning two tragedies which occurred in his lifetime. The way he answered the questions may help us appreciate a perspective on the problem of suffering we can so easily neglect. It is not a complete Christian perspective on the matter, but an important one nevertheless. The account of the incident is found in Luke 13:1-5.

The Occasion

There are two tragic events which provide the occasion for Jesus' response to human suffering.

The first event is man-made, a massacre. The context of the previous chapter is Jesus calling people to read properly the 'signs of the times'. Then, in chapter 13, we read: 'Now there were some present at that time who told Jesus about the Galileans whose blood Pilate had mixed with their sacrifices' (v. 1). For some reason Pilate had ordered the full-scale slaughter of some Galilean Jews, possibly as

---

1. Lyndon Bowring, CARE letter, January, 1995.

they were getting ready for their Passover celebrations. As these people were preparing the Passover lamb, getting ready to come before God on a great religious festival, Roman soldiers under the express command of Pilate had gone on the rampage, killing Jews in Galilee. A monstrous, barbaric act of butchery which would have shocked anyone, equivalent to the so-called ethnic cleansing recently occurring in Bosnia – that is the picture we are to hold in our minds. It was an appalling carnage. Some may have thought that since these were devout people, religious people, who were killed, then God should have afforded them some special protection. Since he evidently did not, then they must have been especially wicked, it was God's judgement on them.

The second event, however, was more of a natural tragedy: a tower block collapsing, crushing eighteen people to death. The victims may have been adults, but there is every possibility that children were included, which would have magnified the tragedy all the more in the minds of Jesus' hearers. This building disaster was as traumatic for the Jews as the Hillsborough football stadium disaster was traumatic for the people of Sheffield and Liverpool or the collapse of that coal tip was traumatic for the people of Aberfan. We are talking about real events and real people – real human suffering. Therefore, understandably, people want to know what does Jesus think regarding tragic situations?

THE RESPONSE OF JESUS

But when Jesus did speak you could have cut the atmosphere with a knife. In our pride we point to human suffering and demand, 'What is God going to do about it?' But Jesus points to human suffering and says, 'What are you going to do about it?' We look at a catastrophe and ask, 'How can God be good?' Jesus looks at a tragedy and asks, 'How can we be so bad?' Underlying the words of Jesus is the rebuke which questions our assumption that we deserve prosperity, peace and blessing (which for the most part we have), but then ignore God until tragedy strikes when we suddenly blame him. No, it's the wrong way around, says Jesus, for what we fail to take in to account is that disaster is precisely what we do deserve and that when tragedy strikes it should cause us not to shake our fist at God but to repent and come to God. The title of this book is 'Why do bad things happen to good people?' We may think that is a fair question. But according to the Bible the real question in the light of the terrible way we treat our Maker and his creation, as well as each other, is why do *good* things happen to bad people? That's the real mystery.

There are three things about Jesus' response which we may find a little shocking. The first is that Jesus does not assume that those who suffered under Pilate or those who were killed by the collapsing tower did not deserve their fate. The fact that he turns to the crowd and urges upon them the truth that unless they repent they *too* will perish shows that Jesus simply assumes that all death is in some way or other the result of sin and is therefore deserved (vv. 3 and 5). This is in line with the whole of the Bible's teaching: 'The day you eat of the forbidden fruit you will surely die,' said God (Gen. 2:17); 'The wages of sin is death,' said Paul (Rom. 6:23). So death, and the tragedy often surrounding it, is God's judicial verdict on our rebellion – we sin, we die.

But if in some way we are to see God's judgement being worked out in human suffering, we are not to go jumping to the wrong conclusions. Here Jesus insists that death by such means is no evidence whatsoever that those who suffer in this way are *more* wicked than those who escape such a fate. Rather the assumption is that we all deserve to die and that if such a thing were to happen to us it would be no less than we deserve: 'Do you think that these Galileans were worse sinners than all the other Galileans because they suffered this way? (v. 2). They *are* sinners, note, according to Jesus. 'Or those eighteen who died when the tower in Siloam fell on them – do you think they were more guilty than all the others living in Jerusalem?' (v. 4). To both questions Jesus gives the answer, 'I tell you, no!' That does not mean that others deserve less, for Jesus says in verse 3: 'But unless you repent, you too will all perish.' This means there is no room for smug moral superiority which we tend to display when something terrible happens to certain people – especially if we have reason not to like them. There is a self-satisfied pronouncement which says, 'What else do you expect with people like that? Serves them right.' We may not always voice it but we do sometimes think it. But Jesus says, 'You think they deserve such treatment; that is nothing to what you deserve.' So we are to show proper humility.

But thirdly we must take seriously the way that Jesus saw wars and natural disasters, not as an opportunity for some abstract philosophical discussion about the goodness of God and his sovereignty, but as an occasion to call men and women to personal repentance. Twice Jesus says that unless we repent – turn from going our own way and turn back to God, which means following Jesus – then we too will perish. This is as certain as night follows day.

This awesome truth is driven home by Jesus with a parable:

> A man had a fig-tree, planted in his vineyard, and he went to look for fruit on it, but did not find any. So he said to the man who took care of the vineyard, 'For three years now I've been coming to look for fruit on this fig-tree and haven't found any. Cut it down! Why should it use up the soil?' 'Sir,' the man replied, 'Leave it alone for one more year, and I'll dig round it and fertilise it. If it bears fruit next year, fine! If not, then cut it down' (vv. 6-9).

Do you see what God is looking for in people and what he will do if he doesn't find it? He is looking for fruit, that is, signs that we have repented and are living lives which reflect a love for him. Primarily, Jesus has Israel in view; for three years they have had Jesus' teaching and ministering, but the time is closing in when it will come to an end and unless there is a response to him then there will be judgement. And that happened, for within forty years Jerusalem was destroyed and Jesus made it quite clear that this would be God's judgement being carried out (Mark 13:2, 28-30). God is as good as his word; if he says a thing he will do it.

Here we have a classic instance of what it means to be 'prophetic'. How is a Christian to be prophetic today? He is prophetic when he brings God's Word to bear on God's world. He is to look at situations through the lens of Scripture and ask 'What is God saying through this, what is God demanding that we do?' And in the case of wars and disasters of this type the answer is always the same: repent, stop thinking that God owes you a favour, stop presuming upon his kindness towards you, and realise what a mess you have made of things, living as a nation or as a church or as an individual without reference to him and his values. Therefore wise up and turn back before it's too late. In other words, suffering should be the occasion for some serious self-examination, asking what lessons must *I* draw from this?

The Second World War came as a shock to many within the churches. A good number of church leaders had imbibed optimistic humanism, really believing that the human race had learnt its lesson from the First World War and that things were going to get better and better every day. They were sincerely of the view that all you had to do with a man like Hitler was to have a nice chat with him and appeal to reason. They had obviously left their Bibles behind (let alone common sense)! So there was utter bewilderment for some when war broke out: How do you explain this? What is a good God doing letting this happen?

There was a man who quite unashamedly told people what was happening, and that was the late Dr Martyn Lloyd-Jones who obviously took Luke 13 seriously. This is what he preached in one of his sermons in 1939 at the outbreak of World War Two:

> God permits and allows such things as war to chastise and punish us; to teach us, and to convict us of our sins, and above all to call us to repentance and acceptance of his gracious offer. The vital question for us therefore is not to ask 'Why does God allow war?' The question for us is to make sure that we are learning the lesson and repenting before God for the sin of our own hearts and the entire human race that leads to such results.[2]

---

2. D. M. Lloyd-Jones, *Why does God allow war?* (Evangelical Press of Wales, 1986).

That is the voice of a prophet.

Isn't it a mark of God's judgement upon us as a nation that we very rarely hear such voices today from amongst our national church leaders? Would it be asking too much, say, of national Christian leaders with access to the media and to the nation to state very simply truths which are basic to the gospel? That there is a God, and we must give an account to him. That he is the only one who can put us right with himself and has done so through the death of his Son, with the resulting call to turn and put our trust in him. I must say that I have not heard that clearly said. And yet we have a social context in this country which literally provides a God-given opportunity for such a call to be made: economic idolatry, rising crime rate, social disintegration. Over the last few years we have had events which have shaken our society to the foundations: open marital infidelity by the royal family, murder by children in Liverpool, the slaughter of children in Dunblane, the stabbing of clergy. What more has to happen for God to get our attention and to shake us into recognising that all is not well? The sheer relevance of the gospel is so obvious.

Let us not misunderstand this. There is no suggestion being made that we should be hard or indifferent to human suffering, far from it. I doubt very much that Jesus said these words without tears in his eyes and sorrow in his voice. But to leave matters solely at the level of sympathy without pointing people to Christ is as callous a thing you can ever do – because we are robbing people of the only hope they have. Can you think of anything more terrible than to escape tragedy in this life only to suffer the greater tragedy of going into a Christless eternity in the next life? Time and time again God is giving people opportunities in the face of human suffering to come back to him. Did you notice in the parable how the period for repentance was extended? That is because of God's love, but that won't go on for ever. We can't keep putting off our response to God, we are to make it now.

I am always amazed and disturbed that people can come to a funeral service – which more than any other occasion should focus minds on eternity, on the shortness of this life and the fact that one day it is going to be our turn to lie in that coffin – and yet leave the service as far away from God's kingdom as when they went in. With every instance of human tragedy there also comes an act of mercy with God calling us to turn and put our trust in him.

What is implicit in what Jesus teaches here is that it is not so much suffering *per se* that is important but our attitude and response to it. David Watson in one of his books gives an example of this with two young fathers. Both had tragically lost children of four or five years of age. One had died of leukaemia; the other had drowned in a swimming pool. One father had been a professing Christian, but was now through his experience a militant atheist. The other father had been an atheist, but through the experience became a Christian. Two similar tragic situations, but two totally different responses. One adding bitterness to despair, the other an opening of the heart to the love and peace that is to be found in Jesus Christ. Jesus is calling for men and women to see that this life is not the be all and end all, that tragedy will come, that we are far from God, reaping only what we have sown. We are called to lay down the arms of rebellion against God and turn back to him as a heavenly Father through the suffering of his Son in our place on the cross.

Chapter 9

SAINTLY SUFFERING

1 Peter 4:12-19

[12] Dear friends, do not be surprised at the painful trial you are suffering, as though something strange were happening to you. [13] But rejoice that you participate in the sufferings of Christ, so that you may be overjoyed when his glory is revealed. [14] If you are insulted because of the name of Christ, you are blessed, for the Spirit of glory and of God rests on you. [15] If you suffer, it should not be as a murderer or thief or any other kind of criminal, or even as a meddler. [16] However, if you suffer as a Christian, do not be ashamed, but praise God that you bear that name. [17] For it is time for judgment to begin with the family of God; and if it begins with us, what will the outcome be for those who do not obey the gospel of God? [18] And, 'If it is hard for the righteous to be saved, what will become of the ungodly and the sinner?'

[19] So then, those who suffer according to God's will should commit themselves to their faithful Creator and continue to do good.

One of the saddest situations that I had to deal with when I was Chaplain at Keele University was that of a young female student. She came to college full of Christian life and enthusiasm. She led several of her friends to a saving faith in Jesus Christ. She was a leader of one of the hall Bible study groups and was tipped as the next vice-president of the student Christian Union. Things could not have looked more promising. But then gradually people began to notice a change. No longer did she bother with the Bible studies. Her attendance at Christian Union meetings and church became more and more irregular, until eventually she stopped going altogether. In fact, she soon began to spend as much time in the student union bar as she used to spend in Christian meetings. She also started a relationship with a non-Christian.

So I was asked to go around to see her. When I eventually met her she was clearly distressed and quite unhappy. I gently asked her concerning the change. Why had she apparently ditched the faith which at one time seemed so precious to her? This is how she replied: 'I have simply become disillusioned. I thought that if you were a Christian then you would always be happy. But I have found things difficult, I have had real struggles and, you know, God doesn't always answer prayer. So I thought, what is the point?'

We may feel some sympathy with what that young woman was saying, especially in the light of so much that passes for evangelism today, when the impression given is that Jesus is some sort of cure for all ills and when so much is made of the blessings of being a Christian, while so little is made of the cost. Where that student went wrong was in thinking that God's supreme concern is simply that we should be happy – free from trouble and feeling good – when the Bible makes it abundantly plain that God's will is that we should be holy, that is, made more and more like Jesus Christ (1 Thess. 4:3).

Can you think of anyone kinder than Jesus? Anyone more loving and compassionate than Jesus? One who was more obedient and content in his relationship to God the Father than Jesus? But also, was there ever a man who was more persecuted than Jesus, who suffered beyond our worst nightmares as he was ridiculed, flogged and then hoisted on a Roman scaffold and held by jagged iron nails? The Bible tells us that 'Jesus learned obedience through what he suffered' (Heb. 5:8).

In other words, in some way, God uses suffering to mould character, which in our case is to get rid of those things which are selfish and to build up endearing qualities such as patience, kindness and understanding. It is certainly my experience that those Christians who have suffered the most, love the most and within them there is an irresistible Christ-likeness. But that Christ-likeness has been achieved at considerable cost.

1 Peter 4:12-19 focuses for us the way in which God will use something like persecution to make Christians into better people. How many times have folk cried out, 'Why is this happening to me, Lord?' One answer to that question is given to us in these verses.

A DIVINE NORM

'Beloved, do not be surprised at the fiery ordeal which comes upon you to prove you, as if something strange were happening to you. But rejoice in so far as you share in Christ's sufferings' (v. 12). What that means is this: the Christian is to expect opposition solely by virtue of the fact that he or she is a follower of Christ. Jesus himself told us as much when he said, 'If the world hates you, keep in mind that it hated me first ... "No servant is greater than his master." If they persecuted me they will persecute you also' (John 15:18-20). Mankind, the Bible often reminds us, is not neutral in its relationship to God, it is in a state of rebellion. If men and women, wanting to rule their own lives without God, cannot attack God directly, then they will do the next best thing and attack his followers.

In the case of Peter's readers that meant violent persecution. It was the practice of Nero to dip Christians in tar and set them alight to illumine his garden parties! There was also the business of throwing them to wild dogs, heating them on grid irons and burning them at the stake. More subtle forms of persecution involved barring them from obtaining employment, which in turn meant that they could not pay their bills, which in turn led to confiscation of property, and when that was exhausted, imprisonment for debt. That is the sort of thing these people were going through.

'But surely,' you say, 'in our society it's a matter of live and let live. Christians would never be subject to that sort of pressure because of their faith?' Really? You tell that to the Jewish boy who becomes a Christian and whose family hold a funeral service for him. You tell that to the nurse who is barred from promotion because she refuses to perform abortions. You suggest that no such persecutions occur to the young man working in the business world who finds his career prospects cut short because he will not engage in shady dealing. For others it may be old friends who point them out and whisper behind their backs: 'What has become of Bill? He has become rather odd lately. He doesn't join in with the dirty jokes at work anymore. He has become a religious crank, you know.' It hurts.

But Peter wants us to realise that when that happens, we are sharing in the sufferings of Christ. In other words, so close and intimate is the relationship between the believer and the risen Jesus that when Christians are attacked, he is being attacked. Remember Jesus' words to Saul on the road to Damascus as he was travelling to arrest Christians and put them in prison: 'Saul, Saul, why do you persecute me?' (Acts 9:4). Saul was persecuting Christians, but in touching them he was touching the apple of Christ's eye. That is why it is a serious thing to abuse Christians.

THE DIVINE PURPOSE

What is more, when the Christian undergoes suffering, especially in the form of persecution, there is a divine purpose behind it: 'the fiery ordeal

... comes upon you in order to prove you' (v. 12); 'For the time has come for judgement [that is, a sifting process] to begin with the household of God [the church]' (v. 17). The idea is that of burning away impurities from a precious metal, or sifting out contaminations in our lives. In short, it is all about purifying us. If you are a believer in Jesus Christ, God so loves you that he is absolutely determined to change you into a creature of such outstanding moral beauty that one day in heaven even the angels will marvel in looking at you. So determined is he to see the rough edges knocked off us that he is willing to use difficulty and opposition as instruments in his skilled hands to do it.

C. S. Lewis describes the way God works:

> When I was a child I often had toothache, and I knew that if I went to my mother she would give me something which would deaden the pain for the night. But I did not go to my mother until the pain became very bad. And the reason I did not go was this. I did not doubt she would give me aspirin; but I knew she would also do something else. I knew she would take me to the dentist the next morning. I could not get what I wanted out of her without getting something more, which I did not want. I knew those dentists; I knew they started fiddling about with all sorts of other teeth which had not begun to ache. They would not let sleeping dogs lie; if you gave them an inch they took a mile. Now, our Lord is like the dentists. If you give him an inch he will take a mile. Dozens of people go to him to be cured of a particular sin which is troubling them. Well, he will do that alright: but he will not stop there. That may be all you asked;

but if you once call him in he will give you the full treatment. That is why he warned people to 'count the cost' before becoming Christians. 'Make no mistake,' he says. 'If you let me in I will make you perfect.'[1]

But how can finding ourselves in difficult circumstances, maybe having someone in our family suddenly struck down ill or having a terrible time at work or being pilloried for being a Christian, be used by God to make us into more godly people? We are told in verse 19: 'Therefore let those who suffer according to God's will do right and entrust their souls to a faithful Creator.' Personally I have found that some of my most intimate, meaningful and precious times with God have been during those times of the most acute difficulty and pain. Yes, I have enjoyed God in the good times, but when I have been knocked sideways, when things happen which make me realise that I have no inner resources of myself, then I am driven to Christ in prayer in an altogether different way. I am *forced* to entrust my soul to the Creator, because he alone can keep it.

Also, it is when things are stripped away from us that we have to exercise faith. It is then we reveal what our true spiritual condition is, and, as Peter says, we are to do right, that is respond in a Christian manner, when things are tough.

---

1. C. S. Lewis, *Mere Christianity* (Fount, 1978).

A very moving example of this was given by the Californian pastor John MacArthur at a conference I attended a few years ago. He told us of some friends of his, a minister and his family, who worked in a small struggling church in Utah in order to win Mormons for Christ.

One day this family phoned MacArthur and said they would like to come down to visit his church and enrol their two lovely teenage daughters at his Bible college. They would be bringing two Italian exchange students along because they were wanting to see them converted. So Dad, Mom, the son, the two teenage daughters and the two Italians set off in their station wagon and arrived on the Saturday. They were excited at the prospect of the Sunday because they wanted to see a big congregation – which in the case of MacArthur's church was a few thousand strong, with large choir and all. They arrived and had a marvellous time of Christian fellowship and blessing. It was pure joy.

But on the return journey home, for some inexplicable reason, the father pulled out too soon at a red light into the intersection just as a large truck was careering down the hill. The truck hit them full speed broad-side. It catapulted the two girls out of the back window of the station wagon on to the kerb, killing them instantly. The son and the two Italians were taken to intensive care with severe internal injuries. The car had almost been cut in half and went up in a fireball, but the parents miraculously survived. What had started off as a day of consummate joy had ended as a holocaust.

As soon as MacArthur arrived at the hospital he went to see the father, and he said to him, 'John, what are your thoughts?' Through tears he replied, 'Well, I keep thinking maybe it's a dream, and I will wake up, but I know that's not true.' And then he said, 'My second thought is this: Isn't God good? He spared those two unsaved Italian boys and took my two Christian girls.' That father knew that his daughters were in the presence of God, he took the Bible seriously – his faith was real. But then he went on and said, 'I wanted my girls to have a big church experience, but I didn't think that it would be this big. And I wanted them to hear a big choir, but I didn't think that it would be the angels.'

Do you see what that man was doing? He was doing what was right, he was entrusting his soul and the souls of his daughters to a faithful Creator. This is proved faith, tested faith, and it came out 100 per cent pure – refined in the crucible of suffering. I defy anyone to explain that except in terms of God at work in that man's life through the Word of God.

But someone might ask, 'Are you saying that suffering, even persecution, is God's will?' I am not saying it, Peter is; it all lies within the orbit of God's permissive will. And if you stop and think about it for a moment, what better comfort could you want than that, that nothing is outside his power?

Is it not consolation to know that because our loving heavenly Father is in control, there is a limit to suffering, both in terms of its intensity and its duration, a limit set by our Creator and Saviour? Isn't there comfort in knowing that in his hands suffering is for our good; purifying us, drawing us closer to himself, so that he can tenderly wipe away the tears from our eyes. But over and above all of these things is there not comfort in knowing that we are not alone when we suffer, but that we can depend upon a *faithful* Creator. I would suggest that indeed there is, and if we lose sight of that, then we will not be able to cope with difficulty in a *Christian* way for a single moment.

This has profound implications for the way in which we view our children. Sometimes we are too over-protective, wanting to shield them too quickly against difficulty. Christian parents, let me ask: do you not look upon your children and wish for them just enough opposition to make them strong, just enough insults to make them choose, just enough hard decisions to make them see that following Jesus involves cost, a cost that is eminently worth it, but still a cost?

THE DIVINE BLESSINGS

Suffering is the sure route to receiving God's blessings:

> Rejoice in so far as you share in Christ's sufferings,
> that you may also rejoice and be glad when his glory

is revealed. If you are reproached for the name of Christ, you are blessed, because the Spirit of glory and of God rests upon you (vv. 13-14).

Isn't that an amazing thing to say? The early Christians considered it a badge of honour to be given a rough time because they owned the name of Christ. It was not a source of acute embarrassment but of joy that they had been counted worthy enough to be following in Christ's footsteps.

Notice how time and time again Peter draws our attention to the future glory which awaits us: 'And after you have suffered a little while, the God of all grace, who called you to his eternal glory in Christ, will himself restore, establish, and strengthen you' (1 Pet. 5:10). If this life is all there is, then of course Christians are mad to embrace suffering. Of course people like that young student will soon become frustrated and disillusioned. But this life is not all there is, nor is it the most important thing. The most important thing is the life to come, 'the eternal weight of glory' believers will experience which will make this life appear to be as nothing more than a dream. That is what awaits us and that is why we have to fix our eyes upon the future, and not see everything in terms of the here and now.

But having said that, we can know something of that joy now even in the suffering. Read Richard Wurmbrand's moving story *Tortured for Christ*.[2]

---

2.   R. Wurmbrand, *Tortured For Christ* (Hodder & Stoughton, 1967).

Wurmbrand was a Romanian pastor who spent many years in communist prisons for his faith. His wife was taken away to a labour camp and they were forced to leave their nine-year-old son to wander the streets. In his book you will read of both the wicked depravity that human beings sink to in their treatment of other human beings, and also of the supremacy of God as you discover that Christian men, who were beaten to a pulp, continued to pray for and preach to their captors. You will be amazed to find Richard Wurmbrand in a cold cell, literally dancing for joy because he has such a sense of the presence of Christ and a taste of heaven in his hell on earth. That is the Spirit of glory at work in the lives of all those who are willing to follow him. The question is: Are we willing?

Chapter 10

THE BIG PICTURE REVISITED

Revelation 5

[1] Then I saw in the right hand of him who sat on the throne a scroll with writing on both sides and sealed with seven seals. [2] And I saw a mighty angel proclaiming in a loud voice, 'Who is worthy to break the seals and open the scroll?' [3] But no-one in heaven or on earth or under the earth could open the scroll or even look inside it. [4] I wept and wept because no-one was found who was worthy to open the scroll or look inside. [5] Then one of the elders said to me, 'Do not weep! See, the Lion of the tribe of Judah, the Root of David, has triumphed. He is able to open the scroll and its seven seals.'

[6] Then I saw a Lamb, looking as if it had been slain, standing in the centre of the throne, encircled by the four living creatures and the elders. He had seven horns and seven eyes, which are the seven spirits of God sent out into all the earth. [7] He came and took the scroll from the right hand of him who sat on the throne. [8] And when he had taken it, the four living creatures and the twenty-four elders fell down before the Lamb. Each one had a harp and they were holding golden bowls full of incense, which are the prayers of the saints. [9] And they sang a new song:

'You are worthy to take the scroll
    and to open its seals,
because you were slain,
    and with your blood you purchased men for God
    from every tribe and language and people and nation.

[10] You have made them to be a kingdom
   and priests to serve our God,
   and they will reign on the earth.'

[11] Then I looked and heard the voice of many angels, numbering thousands upon thousands, and ten thousand times ten thousand. They encircled the throne and the living creatures and the elders. [12] In a loud voice they sang:

'Worthy is the Lamb, who was slain,
   to receive power and wealth and wisdom and strength
   and honour and glory and praise!'

[13] Then I heard every creature in heaven and on earth and under the earth and on the sea, and all that is in them, singing:

'To him who sits on the throne and to the Lamb
   be praise and honour and glory and power,
   for ever and ever!'

[14] The four living creatures said, 'Amen,' and the elders fell down and worshipped.

Maybe, like me, you are a crime-thriller fan. I must admit that I do like to curl up with a good Agatha Christie from time to time. Have you ever noticed how many of these stories turn on what someone accidentally saw, perhaps through a keyhole? It may be the butler who 'just happened' to be stooping down to tie his shoelace, and 'just happened' to spot something strange going on which turns out to be significant. But the problem with looking through keyholes is that you have such a narrow field of vision (not that looking through keyholes is my normal practice!). There may be someone standing just out of sight, or something going on which you cannot see but which, in fact, makes all the difference in the world to your interpretation of things. It seems to me that sometimes Christians engage in what I call keyhole theology, that is, they take a slice of what they know about God or the Bible and mistake it for the whole picture.

For example, in Mark 11:24 Jesus says: 'Whatever you ask for in prayer, believe that you have received it, and it will be yours.' Some have taken this verse as a blank cheque for prayer, as if one can ask for anything, and provided that one has enough faith one is guaranteed to get it, no matter what. It therefore comes as no surprise that disappointment soon sets in when certain prayers aren't answered in the way expected on this basis. What has happened is that one verse has been taken as a keyhole to understanding the whole of prayer and no attention has been given to other biblical passages which stress the sovereignty of God in over-ruling everything; the truth that God is King and therefore has the divine prerogative to turn down some of our prayers or to modify them and give us something better.

In Revelation 5, we have not so much a keyhole but a whole doorway opened for us, a door which reveals the absolute sovereign working of God in the whole of creation through his Son Jesus Christ.

THE THRONE WHICH IS AT THE CENTRE
Before we take a look at this amazing passage in detail, it might be helpful to say a few words about

understanding the Book of Revelation in general. Let's face it, this is a book that has been a fertile breeding ground for the cults, providing ample material to supply their way-out beliefs. People so easily go astray when turning to this book and the main reason for this is a failure to realise the *type* of book it is. It is not a religious cryptic crossword puzzle designed to occupy the minds of those who have time on their hands. It is a pastoral letter written to Christians who were literally being torn apart because of their faith. Using powerful imagery, most of which comes from the Old Testament, it is a book intended to be a source of comfort to believers who are finding life almost unbearable. The style of writing, which is called apocalyptic, may seem obscure and unusual to us, but at the time when John wrote it (in the AD 90s) and for a century or so before, this was familiar territory for many. The symbolism, especially the use of numbers, was common fare for those used to handling this particular literary genre.

The one unmistakable message of this book which is repeated over and over again is 'Your God reigns'. That is what the Book of Revelation is primarily about. Nothing happens by chance, whether it be on the broader canvas of world history or the much smaller scene of the Christian's personal life. Instead, God through his Son is bringing about his eternal purposes for our ultimate good and his supreme glory, *although* at times it may not seem like it. And it is because it sometimes doesn't seem like it that we are taken with John behind the scenes, as it were, to see what is presently hidden from us.

The setting, which is introduced in chapter 4, is as follows: John in his vision has a door opened to him into the invisible spiritual world, the heavenly realms. Straightaway he sees the throne of God, a throne which pulsates light and glory, and occupies the centre of everything. Surrounding the throne are the twenty-four elders which one can take to represent the whole people of God, both Old and New Testaments – the twelve tribes of Israel and the twelve apostles. We then glimpse the living creatures in verse 6; and there are four, symbolising the four corners of the earth. So just as the twenty-four elders represent God ruling over his people, the four creatures represent God ruling over his creation. Nothing lies outside his power and purpose, everything is created by him and for him:

> You are worthy, our Lord and God,
> > to receive glory and honour and power,
> for you created all things,
> > and by your will they were created
> > and have their being (4:11).

However, this is the God who is not only at the centre of the universe, but graciously sits enthroned in the centre of his people, even as they meet. Now there's a surprise. Or at least it would have been, say, to a young eighteen-year-old Jewish Christian whom we shall call Judith from the little church in Smyrna when she heard about this book. In AD 95, because of her faith, she occupies a prison cell. Her family who are Jewish won't have anything to do with her. They cannot understand why she has left all that Judaism has to offer to worship a crucified carpenter from Nazareth. And from where she is lying, cold and hungry, it is the Roman Emperor Domitian who seems to be securely seated on *his* throne, calling the shots. But no. For according to this vision, this Jewish Christian girl is, as far as God is concerned, touching the very edge of the divine throne. God loves her, he is still watching out for her interests and he is in control. Do we believe that? It is a mighty belief to have, and it is a belief that has brought untold comfort to countless Christians down the ages as they faced the most appalling situations.

THE FUTURE WHICH IS SECURE

But you say: 'What concerns me is the future. God may be the Creator and Sustainer of all things, but can we be certain that future events will not get out of hand? Why, I'm afraid to switch on the news these days because things seem to be getting worse.' Do you ever feel like that? If so, then Revelation 5 contains a message for you; for it is all about the question of God securing the future:

> Then I saw in the right hand of him who sat on
> the throne a scroll with writing on both sides and

sealed with seven seals. And I saw a mighty angel proclaiming in a loud voice, 'Who is worthy to break the seals and open the scroll?' But no-one in heaven or on earth or under the earth could open the scroll or even look inside it. I wept and wept because no-one was found who was worthy to open the scroll or look inside (vv. 1-4).

The right hand of God always indicates his rule and the good purpose he wants to achieve. The scroll in his right hand is a legal document with writing on both sides, sealed with seven seals. The very nature of the document suggests its content and purpose, namely, that it is God's plan, God's royal decree with respect to the whole of history. But there is a problem and the problem is this: the document is sealed with seven seals (the number of completeness/wholeness) and if it is not opened, not only will God's will not be revealed, it won't be carried out. In other words, the opening of the seals is necessary both for the revelation and the activation of God's decree.

So in verse 2 the cry goes out in a loud voice, with such volume that it echoes throughout the universe in the hope that there might just be someone who can do it: 'Who is worthy to break the seals and open the scroll?'

Try to feel the heightening tension of the strained silence which follows, with the creatures of heaven waiting, hoping, praying that there will be an answer, and then the utter despair and panic which ensues: 'But no-one in heaven or on earth or under the earth could open the scroll or even look inside it.' John wept and wept because no-one was found.

Have you ever had a nightmare where something dreadful is happening to you and you are trying to cry out but your voice is silent, and you suddenly wake up only to find yourself weeping? That is how John is feeling here. But why? Well, think through the implications. If this scroll is not opened, God's plan will not be carried out. The world will not be governed in the interests of God and his people. There will be no judgement, no righting of wrongs, no ultimate triumph of good over evil. Men like Hitler, Stalin and all the butchers who have appeared throughout history, and even the devil himself, will get away with everything. In short, if God can't bring about his purpose for the world, then there is no hope of justice whatsoever. Is not that precisely the tragic situation of those who live lives without God, who believe that we live in a universe with no real meaning, but that it is all one great cosmic accident? They may try to make the best of a bad job, but at the end of the day there is no ultimate difference between the Yorkshire Ripper and Mother Teresa, they both die, and the world eventually comes to nothing. That is the only logical outcome of unbelief: 'Eat, drink and be merry for tomorrow we die.' It is tragic, if there is no God.

But then something happens in verse 5 which is the answer to John's predicament and indeed mankind's predicament. One is found who can open the scroll and bring about the ultimate victory of good over evil: 'Do not weep!' says the elder. 'See, the Lion of the tribe of Judah, the Root of David, has triumphed. He is able to open the scroll and its seven seals.'

And who is this person? It is the Lord Jesus.

THE LION WHO IS THE LAMB

Can you imagine John's utter amazement when he looks up expecting to see a Lion, that majestic beast symbolising royalty and power, only to glimpse a Lamb, weak, limping as if it had been butchered: 'Then I saw a Lamb, looking as if it had been slain, standing in the centre of the throne, encircled by the four living creatures and the elders' (v. 6). The contrast could not be greater. And yet, the two are one and the same. For Jesus Christ who is now seated in heaven above every rule and authority, clothed in splendour and majesty, occupies that position precisely because he first suffered and died on a cross. Even in heaven he still bears the scars of his death, the nail-pierced hands, the wounded side. The Lion is the Lamb. Jesus gave his life as a sacrificial lamb to wash away the filth of our sin and to turn aside God's anger from us by taking it to himself and so conquering sin, death and the devil. He is all-ruling and all-knowing as indicated by the seven horns (horns denoting rule) and seven eyes (indicating total omniscience). There is no-one else worthy or able to reveal and execute the will of God the Father but Jesus alone, hence the praise given to him in verse 9:

> You are worthy to take the scroll
>   and to open its seals,
> because you were slain,
>   and with your blood you purchased men for God from
> every tribe and language and people and nation.

Jesus lived in utter obedience and love to his Father, even to the point of dying a death that he did not deserve so that poor sinners like you and I might taste eternal life. Someone like that is not only worthy to rule for God but able. You can trust someone like that to do right. It is amazing how throughout history people have been looking for leaders, role models, someone to follow – the Bible says look no further, the ultimate leader, Jesus Christ, has come.

THE PLAN WHICH IS PERFECTED

The question which must come to our minds on reading this is, 'Why is it necessary for someone to open the scroll and carry out God's plans? Why should not God do it himself, after all he is God?' The answer to that question lies in what the Bible teaches us about God's original intention for his world. In Genesis 1 and 2 we see that it was God's plan to rule and care for his world through a man. But Adam and the rest of us ever since have thwarted that design by turning our backs on God, trying to act as if we were gods, and a fine mess we have made of things too! But God was going to fulfil his original intention of having one man who would reign over his creation under him, but who first would rescue it, bringing people to surrender their lives to him in love, and that was the God-man, Jesus Christ.

This is the way the writer to the Hebrews puts it:

> It is not to angels that he has subjected the world to come, about which we are speaking. But there is a place where someone has testified:
> 'What is man that you are mindful of him,
>   the son of man that you care for him?
> You made him a little lower than the angels;
>   you crowned him with glory and honour
>   and put everything under his feet.'
>
> In putting everything under him, God left nothing that is not subject to him. Yet at the present we do not see everything subject to him. But we see Jesus, who was made a little lower than the angels, now crowned with glory and honour because he suffered death, so that by the grace of God he might taste death for everyone (2:5-9).

We don't see everything subjected to him as yet, but Jesus is still on the throne and by faith we see him there, guiding, directing, weaving all events according to his unsearchable wisdom until one day when he will return and wind up the whole drama, righting every kind of wrong, and taking his followers to be with him in the 'world to come' for ever. Now there's a future to look forward to!

Listen to the way the apostle Paul develops the same thought in Romans 8:28: 'We know that in all things God works for the good of those who love him, who have been called according to his purpose'. That is what Revelation 5 is getting at. God is working all things through Christ to the good of those who love him (the 'good' being the conformity to the image of Jesus, as he goes on to say in verse 29). All things? What, even the pain, the difficulties? That's what he says.

Reflecting on God sovereignly using suffering to sanctify his people, the great hymn writer and former slave trader, John Newton, wrote these words:

> I asked the Lord that I might grow
> In faith and love, and every grace,
> Might more of his salvation know
> And seek more earnestly his face.
>
> 'Twas he who taught me thus to pray,
> And he, I trust, has answered prayer;
> But it has been in such a way
> As almost drove me to despair.
>
> I hoped that in some favoured hour
> At once he'd answer my request;
> And by his love's constraining power;
> Subdue my sins and give me rest.
>
> Instead of this, he made me feel
> The hidden evils of my heart,
> And let the angry powers of hell
> Assault my soul in every part.
>
> Yea, more, with his own hand he seemed
> Intent to aggravate my woe,

Crossed all the fair designs I schemed
Blasted my gourds, and laid me low.

'Lord, why is this?' I trembling cried,
'Wilt thou pursue thy worm to death?'
''Tis in this way,' the Lord replied,
'I answer prayer for grace and faith.

'These inward trials I employ
From self and pride to set thee free,
And break thy schemes of earthly joy,
That thou mayest seek thy all in me.'

When we believe that (and only the Christian can believe it), then it becomes possible to look at life and the world through different eyes. Though pain is still present (as it will always be in this fallen world), however wavering, however feeble we may feel, it is possible by God's grace to face life with a quiet assurance and certainty that God will do what is right. We do not know what the future holds, but we do know the one who holds the future – the Lamb who is on the throne.

Christian Focus Publications

publishes books for all ages
Our mission statement -

STAYING FAITHFUL

In dependence upon God we seek to impact the world through literature faithful to his infallible word, the Bible. Our aim is to ensure that the Lord Jesus Christ is presented as the only hope to obtain forgiveness of sin, live a useful life and look forward to heaven with Him.

REACHING OUT

Christ's last command requires us to reach out to our world with His gospel. We seek to help fulfil that by publishing books that point people towards Jesus and help them develop a Christ-like maturity. We aim to equip all levels of readers for life, work, ministry and mission.

Books in our adult range are published in three imprints:

Christian Focus contains popular works including biographies, commentaries, basic doctrine and Christian living. Our children's books are also published in this imprint.

Mentor focuses on books written at a level suitable for Bible College and seminary students, pastors, and other serious readers. The imprint includes commentaries, doctrinal studies, examination of current issues and church history.

Christian Heritage contains classic writings from the past.

Christian Focus Publications Ltd
Geanies House, Fearn, Ross-shire,
IV20 1TW, Scotland, United Kingdom.
info@christianfocus.com
www.christianfocus.com